The Womb Remembers

The Womb Remembers

A Lived Experience of Prenatal Rejection and the Search for Belonging

Barbara Sharp

Foreword by Melissa Varner

RESOURCE *Publications* · Eugene, Oregon

Resource Publications
An Imprint of Wipf and Stock Publishers
199 W. 8th Ave., Suite 3
Eugene, OR 97401

www.wipfandstock.com

PAPERBACK ISBN: 979-8-3852-6556-5
HARDCOVER ISBN: 979-8-3852-6557-2
EBOOK ISBN: 979-8-3852-6558-9

VERSION NUMBER 12/10/25

To my daughters—thank you for your patience, love, and grace as I healed, grew, and found my voice. You are part of my redemption story. To my dissertation advisors—Dr. Laurens Vansluytman and Dr. I. Tophoven—thank you for your guidance, wisdom, and belief in this deeply personal work. To the courageous participants who shared their stories—your honesty lit the way for this book. To every reader who picks up these pages—may you find language for your wounds and hope for your healing. And to my God—You saw me before my first breath, loved me in the secret of the womb, and declared me worthy. All of this is for Your glory.

Contents

Foreword

FROM THE VERY FIRST moment I met Dr. Barbara Sharp, I sensed something truly special about her. We first crossed paths during a season when she was intentionally seeking her own healing through an extended inner-healing journey that required travel and deep personal reflection. Even then, it was evident that she carried a profound hunger for truth and freedom—qualities that would later become hallmarks of her life and ministry.

Dr. Sharp possesses a rare gift: the ability to listen deeply and to speak words of truth directly into the hidden places of the heart. What makes her voice even more powerful is that she first welcomes those truths into her own life. Out of her personal journey has come a rich harvest, one that she now generously shares with others.

Dr. Sharp has walked through her own valleys and emerged with treasures of wisdom that could only be discovered through pain transformed by grace. She does not write as a distant observer but as one who has tasted the sting of rejection and the sweetness of redemption. Her life and work are both testimony and invitation—proof that healing is possible, and that God specializes in rewriting stories that once seemed beyond repair.

In *The Womb Remembers*, Dr. Sharp offers a deeply courageous and groundbreaking work. With clinical insight and spiritual discernment, she explores the earliest and often unspoken experiences that shape our sense of belonging and identity. It takes courage to enter such sacred territory, yet she does so with reverence and clarity, illuminating what happens when love is withheld before birth and showing how divine love steps in to restore what was lost.

What makes this book truly remarkable is the way Dr. Sharp brings together her years of professional practice, her theological understanding, and her personal encounters with God to reveal that true healing engages the whole person—mind, body, and soul. In our conversations, I have heard her share about her counseling approach and the thoughtful, holistic ways she helps others move toward wholeness. Her compassion and wisdom are unmistakable, and the same intentional care she offers in conversation shines through in her writings. *The Womb Remembers* is more than a book—it is a movement toward wholeness. It speaks to the parts of us that were silenced long ago and invites us to believe that even the earliest wounds can be touched by grace. Each story is a reminder that love still has the final word and that healing is both possible and personal.

I believe this message will meet every reader at a deeply personal place. Whether approaching it from a lens of faith, psychology, or simply human longing, these pages invite reflection, courage, and renewal. The truths within will resonate with anyone who has ever questioned their worth or wondered if the pain of their beginning could ever lead to peace.

My prayer is that this work will help you rediscover your worth, reframe your pain, and rest in the truth that you have always been known and loved by your Creator. May these pages lead you closer to the One who remembers every detail of your beginning and promises to make all things new.

—Melissa Varner
Elijah House Prayer Counselor

Preface

THIS BOOK WAS BORN out of both study and deep personal ache. For years, I carried wounds I could not name, only to discover much later that their roots reached back before I ever drew my first breath. My own story of being unwanted in the womb set me on a lifelong journey of searching for love, belonging, and healing.

In my work as a therapist and in my walk with Christ, I have encountered many others who bear the same invisible mark of rejection. Their lives, though different in detail, echo the same silent wound that whispers, *"You were never meant to be."* This book gives voice to that wound and testifies to the One who heals it.

My prayer is that these pages will not only offer understanding but also awaken hope. If you, too, have ever questioned your worth or wrestled with belonging, I want you to know this: you are not alone, and your story does not end with rejection.

It is my deepest desire that *The Womb Remembers* will serve as both a mirror and a lamp—reflecting the hidden pain of prenatal rejection and illuminating the path toward healing, restoration, and the embrace of God's unfailing love.

—Dr. Barbara Sharp

Author's Note

*Psychology, Scripture, and the
Work of the Holy Spirit*

WHEN I BEGAN MY counseling journey, I wrestled deeply with how
to bring my faith into the clinical space. Most modern psychology
is rooted in humanistic philosophy, which elevates human reason as
the ultimate standard of truth and often excludes faith, the supernat-
ural, and Scripture. From that perspective, people are viewed as ba-
sically good and capable of finding all the answers to their problems
within themselves. The Bible presents a different picture. Humanity
is created in God's image (Genesis 1:26; 2:7), yet deeply affected by
sin (Ephesians 2:1; Jeremiah 17:9). True healing and transformation
involve more than behavior modification or emotional insight; they
require spiritual renewal through Jesus Christ.

For years, I tried to apply secular interventions that addressed
thoughts and behaviors but left the spiritual root untouched. Over
time, I came to see that God Himself had directed me to pursue
my degree in counseling—not to replace faith with psychology, but
to integrate the two under His guidance. I attended a Christian
college where Scripture and sound psychological principles were
woven together. This integration became a bridge: professional
tools helped me understand human development and trauma,
while God's Word and the work of the Holy Spirit brought lasting transformation. Ultimately, it is not theory or technique that
changes a heart—it is the living relationship with Jesus Christ. As

that relationship deepens, the Holy Spirit cultivates *the fruit of the Spirit* in us:

> But the fruit of the Spirit is love, joy, peace, patience, kindness, goodness, faithfulness, gentleness, and self-control. Against such things there is no law.
> —*Galatians 5:22–23*

Psychological insights can support growth, but they cannot replace the transforming power of God. Biblical truth remains the foundation; clinical knowledge can serve as a tool—but never the source—of healing. My work and writing flow from this conviction: spiritual formation and emotional healing are not opposing paths—they are meant to converge under the guidance of Christ.

Confidentiality Disclaimer

THE STORIES SHARED IN this book are drawn from my years of clinical practice, personal experience, and research. In every instance, names and identifying details have been changed to protect the privacy of individuals. In some cases, composite stories have been created by blending elements from multiple client experiences.

Any resemblance to actual persons, living or deceased, is purely coincidental. These stories are presented not as biographical accounts, but as illustrations of themes related to trauma, rejection, healing, and restoration. My foremost commitment is to honor the dignity of those I serve while offering insights that may bring hope and understanding to others.

Introduction

THERE ARE WOUNDS THAT cry out long before words are ever spoken—wounds formed in silence, buried deep beneath our awareness, yet shaping how we love, connect, and see ourselves. This book is about one such wound: the ache of being unwanted before birth.

Prenatal rejection—the experience or awareness of being unwanted or unplanned during pregnancy—has received little attention in social work or trauma research. For much of my life, I could not name this ache. I only knew the emptiness, the fear of rejection, and the longing to be seen and loved. It wasn't until my own healing journey began—both as a woman and as a therapist—that I came to understand a profound truth: *the womb remembers.*

This work began as a scholarly investigation, a dissertation intended to give voice to those born from unwanted pregnancies. Yet in time it became more than research, for the participants I interviewed entrusted me with fragments of their souls. Each one bravely revealed the deep imprint left upon their lives by the knowledge—spoken or unspoken—that they were not wanted in the womb.

Despite decades of research on attachment and early trauma, prenatal experiences remain an understudied domain. Emerging evidence suggests that feelings of rejection or neglect before birth may contribute to later struggles with self-worth, identity formation, and relationships.

The stories of the participants I interviewed are raw, sacred, and deeply human. They speak of shame, confusion, survival, and search—and yet also of grace, resilience, and the gradual uncovering of identity. As I listened, I heard echoes of my own story. I realized how many of us—regardless of background—carry hidden wounds from our earliest beginnings.

This research seeks to fill a gap in the literature by illuminating the connections between prenatal emotional environments and later mental health outcomes such as anxiety, depression, and attachment difficulties. But it is also more than research. This book is written for those who have struggled to feel worthy of love, for those who have tried to fill the void with performance, perfectionism, people-pleasing, or numbing pain. It is for those who still wonder, deep down: *Was I ever truly wanted?*

To provide a fuller understanding of these complex experiences, this manuscript integrates psychological theory with biblical insight, offering a holistic framework for understanding prenatal rejection. By bridging these perspectives, the work seeks to inform both clinical practice and Christian spiritual care, enriching approaches to healing and resilience.

Through clinical insight, biblical reflection, and lived narratives, *The Womb Remembers* explores the emotional and psychological impact of prenatal rejection. More importantly, it points toward healing—not through blame or bitterness, but through compassionate care and a deeper understanding of self.

You are not a mistake. Your life is not incidental. Even if you were not planned or welcomed by human hands, you have always been known and valued. May these pages help you find language for your ache and courage for your healing.

Literature Review

Understanding Prenatal Rejection
and Its Lifelong Impact

THE WOMB'S EMOTIONAL AND psychological environment has long been understood as vital to early development. Researchers have studied maternal stress, trauma, and ambivalence during pregnancy, yet one critical gap remains: the voices of those born from unwanted pregnancies. This review brings together key clinical and academic studies on prenatal experience, maternal–infant bonding, and the lasting effects of early prenatal rejection—laying the groundwork for the stories that follow.

Unwanted Pregnancy and Maternal Well-being

A substantial body of research has investigated the impact of unwanted pregnancy on maternal emotional and physical health. Women who carry unwanted pregnancies often report higher levels of depression, anxiety, and perceived stress during gestation, as well as less positive attitudes toward motherhood. These experiences of abuse are significantly associated with unintended pregnancies, and unintended pregnancies have been linked in broader research to inadequate prenatal care, substance use, and diminished maternal–fetal bonding, which in turn influence fetal development and birth outcomes. Most studies on the prenatal environment focus only on the mother's or infant's physical health.

However, very few explore how this environment shapes the developing baby's emotional well-being and their ability to form attachments later in life.

David et al.[1] raised the central question: *"What is the fate of a child born from an unwanted pregnancy?"* For many years, clinicians believed that unwantedness heightened vulnerability to later emotional and psychological distress. The Prague Study, conducted by David and colleagues, sought to test this premise through long-term, systematic investigation. Conducted in the 1960s, when abortion was illegal in Czechoslovakia, it followed children whose mothers had sought but were denied abortions.

These "born unwanted" children were tracked for decades into adulthood and consistently demonstrated higher rates of depression, psychiatric hospitalization, and social difficulties compared to peers who had been planned and welcomed. Many struggled academically and relationally, with some experiencing higher involvement in the criminal justice system.

This landmark study underscored that the experience of being unwanted in the womb is not quickly outgrown; it lingers, shaping development, identity, and the way individuals relate to the world. With this foundation, other research turned to prenatal stress and fetal development to explore how maternal emotional states further influence the unborn child.

The Turnaway Study

In recent years, one of the most widely discussed investigations into unwanted pregnancy outcomes has been the Turnaway Study, conducted by UCSF's Advancing New Standards in Reproductive Health (ANSIRH) program. This longitudinal project followed nearly 1,000 women who either received an abortion or were denied one because they were past the gestational limit. The researchers concluded that abortion itself did not increase long-term rates of depression, anxiety, or suicidality.[2] Instead, they

1. David et al., "Born Unwanted 25 Years Later."
2. Foster et al., *The Turnaway Study.*

emphasized that women denied abortions faced more immediate hardship, including economic strain, health complications, and unstable relationships.

Other research has reached different conclusions. Several meta-analyses and cohort studies[3] have associated abortion with increased risks of depression, substance abuse, and suicidality, underscoring the complexity of the psychological outcomes linked to unwanted pregnancy.

Note to the Reader

If this part of the research feels heavy, you are not alone. Abortion touches many lives, often in silence. Behind the statistics are real people—women, men, and families—carrying grief that may never be seen. Abortion itself is one of the most painful expressions of rejection: the rejection of a life not yet lived, and often the rejection of self that lingers afterward. If you have walked this road yourself, hear this: your story is not beyond God's mercy. His compassion runs deeper than regret, and His healing can reach even the places marked by shame or sorrow. The wound of rejection may leave its mark, but it does not have to define the rest of your life. In Christ, there is always the promise of restoration, forgiveness, and a new beginning.

Taken together, these studies highlight what is at the heart of this book: whether through unwanted birth or abortion, the wound of prenatal rejection leaves a lasting imprint. While clinical research may differ in its conclusions, the lived experiences of those who carry this wound testify to its reality—and to the desperate need for healing.

Recent work adds another layer of evidence. The Amsterdam Born Children and Their Development (ABCD) study is a large, ongoing birth cohort in the Netherlands. Though it did not directly measure unwanted pregnancies, its findings are striking: children whose mothers experienced high stress while carrying them were more likely to later struggle with anxiety, sadness, and

---

3. Fergusson et al.; Coleman; Reardon & Cougle.

behavioral difficulties. Stress in the womb may not always stem from rejection, but when rejection is present—whether spoken or silent—it magnifies the weight the child carries.

That early rejection echoes through emotional development, shaping how a person relates to themselves and others.

Yet these outcomes were not fixed. Maternal bonding after birth, along with the mother's own mental health, could either soften or intensify the impact. This reinforces what both clinical research and lived narratives of prenatal rejection reveal: the womb experience leaves a silent imprint—one that later environments can either buffer or magnify. For children carried under the shadow of unwantedness, that beginning often writes a quiet story that shapes their sense of self and relationship to the world.

Prenatal Stress and Fetal Development

Emerging research in developmental psychology and neurobiology reveals that the fetus is not a passive recipient in utero but an active responder to maternal emotional states. Studies such as *Maternal Prenatal Stress Phenotypes Associate with Fetal Neurodevelopment and Birth Outcomes* demonstrate that elevated maternal cortisol and emotional distress during pregnancy are linked to alterations in fetal brain development, lower birth weight, and later emotional dysregulation.[4]

For many expectant mothers, chronic racial discrimination operates as a unique stressor—one that wears on both mind and body, with lasting consequences for pregnancy and birth outcomes. Research shows that repeated experiences of racism can elevate maternal stress hormones, causing biological changes that influence the developing baby. These disruptions in the body's stress response—such as increased cortisol and the gradual "wear and tear" known as allostatic load—may help explain how trauma imprints itself biologically and extends across generations.

---

4. Zijlmans et al., "Maternal Prenatal Stress Phenotypes."

The Wounds from the Womb: Early Emotional Encoding

The theory that emotional wounds can be encoded before birth has been echoed by clinicians, psychologists, and Christian spiritual counselors. Thomas Verny—psychiatrist, psychologist, and founding president of the Association for Pre- and Perinatal Psychology and Health—along with writer Pamela Weintraub, contend that prenatal maternal emotions profoundly influence the unborn child's experiential environment.

Psychologist David Chamberlain likewise suggests that an unborn child may internalize maternal ambivalence or rejection as forms of shame, fear, or a sense of not belonging. These early imprints can become the root of emotional struggles that surface in adolescence and adulthood. In this context, the question shifts from "Can the fetus feel unwanted?" to "What are the lasting consequences of being unwanted?"

According to Cortizo,[5] the Calming Womb Family Therapy Model advocates that therapeutic intervention with expectant mothers should begin during pregnancy and be conceptualized as family therapy that includes the unborn baby as an active participant. Cortizo explains[6] that "the healing of the pregnant mother functions as a preventive measure and intervention for her baby."

The model emphasizes that bonding should begin at conception, with mothers, fathers, and medical professionals working together to support the womb baby's emotional development. Prenatal and perinatal psychotherapy is described as *"the therapy of the future,"* where caring for the mother is understood as inseparable from caring for the child. Beyond clinical insight, this truth reminds us that when a mother tends to her own wounds, she spares her child from carrying them. Put simply, when the mother heals, the child does not have to heal from her.

---

5. Cortizo, "The Calming Womb Family Therapy Model."
6. Cortizo, "The Calming Womb Family Therapy Model." 128.

Attachment Theory and Early Identity Formation

John Bowlby's attachment theory provides a foundational framework for understanding how early relational experiences shape identity and emotional resilience. When a child's earliest experience—even prior to birth—is one of prenatal rejection, it may result in an insecure attachment style, diminished self-worth, and lifelong relational challenges. An insecure attachment style simply means that the child grows up uncertain if their needs for love, safety, and connection will be met, which can shape how they relate to others throughout life.

Although Bowlby and Ainsworth[7] focused primarily on postnatal bonding, more recent studies expand attachment theory to include prenatal factors. When attachment is disrupted in the womb, the infant's developing capacity for trust and emotional connection may be weakened, setting the stage for difficulties in forming secure relationships later on.

What the Womb Baby Needs

If we believe that emotional imprinting begins before birth, then the way we care for the unborn child must be intentional and tender. According to Cortizo,[8] the womb baby needs more than just biological survival—they need emotional and sensory engagement that fosters safety and belonging. These simple, mindful interactions can serve as the foundation for secure attachment and long-term emotional well-being:

- To be talked to and greeted regularly
- For the mother to narrate shared activities
- To be read to, sung to, and danced with

---

7. Bowlby, A Secure Base; Ainsworth, "Object Relations, Dependency, and Attachment."

8. Cortizo, "The Calming Womb Family Therapy Model," 130.

- To experience mindfulness through the mother's calm presence
- To hear words of love from caregivers
- To feel wanted and released from emotional responsibility
- To engage in walking (indoors on a treadmill or outdoors in nature)
- To share in peaceful, meditative moments with the mother
- To be acknowledged and welcomed joyfully at birth

These early gestures of connection speak to the unborn child's developing sense of self and belonging. They also affirm that even babies who were initially unplanned or unwanted can be emotionally received, nurtured, and healed—starting in the womb.

Therapist Insight

I once encouraged a young African American mother to engage in many of the nurturing behaviors listed above—talking to her baby, singing, sharing peaceful moments together. She looked at me and said bluntly, "Only white people do that." Her words revealed more than reluctance; they exposed a generational silence around emotional attunement in some communities of color—born out of survival, trauma, and social conditioning. But healing cannot remain a cultural luxury—it must become a generational necessity. These practices are not race-specific; they are life-affirming. Every child—regardless of race, class, or culture—deserves to be welcomed, loved, and emotionally embraced, starting in the womb.

I've also seen the blessing that comes from intentional womb connection. My sister, for example, made it a daily practice to read aloud to her unborn baby during pregnancy. That child, now older, is an avid reader—curious, expressive, and emotionally aware. Her story is a reminder that what we speak, sing, or share in the womb can leave a lasting imprint. The womb is a sacred space—not only for physical development, but also for emotional and relational imprinting. When we speak life into our children from the beginning, we lay the foundation for resilience, trust, and belonging.

Gaps in the Literature: The Missing Voice of the Child

While clinical studies have robustly documented maternal experiences of stress, trauma, and rejection during pregnancy, far less attention has been paid to the retrospective narratives of those who were born from unwanted pregnancies. How does it feel to learn—explicitly or implicitly—that your life was unplanned, unwelcomed, or resisted? What psychological, emotional, or spiritual scars might that knowledge leave behind? Most psychological research emphasizes the parent's perspective or early childhood behavior.

Very few studies follow the child's story into adulthood, let alone capture the deeply personal impact of this early rejection on identity formation, emotional development, and spiritual well-being. This book seeks to fill that void. By amplifying the lived experiences of adults who were born from pregnancies marked by prenatal rejection, it bridges clinical science with personal narrative and invites a more compassionate, holistic understanding of prenatal trauma and its enduring effects.

Current Clinical Implications and the Urgency for Prenatal Psychotherapy

Despite the silence surrounding the long-term effects of prenatal rejection, many expectant mothers—especially those considered high-risk—are open to therapeutic support when it offers tools for emotional bonding and practical preparation. Services like couple's therapy, prenatal education, and stress-reduction practices such as guided relaxation and prayer provide a strong foundation for womb-parenting. Yet, when developmental attachment wounds, traumatic histories, or environmental stressors remain unresolved, pregnancy itself can reopen deep emotional pain. Fraiberg, Adelson, and Shapiro described these unhealed wounds as "the ghost in the nursery," underscoring how parents may unconsciously replay their own past traumas in early caregiving interactions.[9]

In these moments, psychotherapy is not just treatment—it is prevention. Early intervention through pre-perinatal counseling[10] has the potential to disrupt intergenerational cycles of neglect, trauma, and shame. As pregnancy becomes both a vulnerable and transformative window, targeted therapeutic care equips mothers to bond with their babies while healing themselves. The future of womb-based healing lies in recognizing that treating the mother is also treating the child—emotionally, relationally, and spiritually.

Inheriting the Ache: Intergenerational Trauma and the Womb

Some wounds are passed down not through words, but through silence. Not through stories, but through sensations—carried unknowingly in the womb, written into the body before a child ever takes their first breath. This hidden ache of intergenerational trauma is something I later recognized in my own story. I did not understand why I felt so disconnected in my relationship with my mother—and in so many other relationships—until it was revealed to me that I had been born unwanted, rejected from the womb. I hadn't carried that knowledge as a belief; I simply lived with a deep ache I could not name.

Once the truth came to light, everything began to make sense. It wasn't until I began my own healing journey that I discovered the ache began long before I was born. My mother, too, had been unwanted. She carried a wound of rejection she never spoke about, but it lived in her body and her soul, shaping how she saw herself—and, unknowingly, how she saw me. Studies indicate

---

9. Fraiberg, Adelson, and Shapiro, "Ghosts in the Nursery."
10. Nichols and Schwartz, *Family Therapy*.

that trauma leaves biological imprints which can extend across generations.

As I sought counseling, I came across a therapist who worked primarily with the "here and now," using the Gestalt approach, which emphasizes present awareness and immediate coping. That framework helped me survive in the moment, but it did not explain the deep ache I carried. Years later, with a second therapist, I was finally invited to explore the root issues. Only then did I begin to see that my struggles weren't random; they were connected to wounds that had begun long before I was born.

One of my professors once told me, "Knowing the root issue does not guarantee change." Awareness is only the beginning. Transformation comes when the wound is not just identified but cared for—through grace, through truth, and through the daily practice of walking in the identity God has given us.

When I became a mother, I discovered this reality firsthand. I loved my daughter deeply, yet something within me remained blocked. There was fear, distance, an invisible wall I could not explain. Later, as I grew in self-awareness and studied trauma and attachment, I realized I had repeated what I had received. The wound had passed from my mother to me—and from me to my daughter.

This generational transmission of pain is not unique to my story. Increasing research in both psychology and neurobiology suggests that trauma can be biologically and emotionally passed down through generations. Yehuda et al.[11] found that the adult children of Holocaust survivors carried changes in a gene that regulates stress. These changes—known as epigenetic markers—suggest that a parent's trauma can leave biological imprints that are passed down to the next generation. Attachment researchers have long noted that unresolved maternal trauma can become a barrier to secure bonding with one's own child.

---

11. Yehuda et al., 'Holocaust Exposure Induced Intergenerational Effects on FKBP5 Methylation,' 372.

Note to the Reader

If you have felt a heaviness that seemed larger than your own story, you are not imagining it. Sometimes the pain we carry began long before we entered the world. Family wounds can echo across generations, shaping how we see ourselves and how we relate to others. Even in utero, stress and emotional rejection can alter a developing fetus's neurobiology.

As Thomas Verny observed, the womb is the first classroom, and the lessons are often written in fear, abandonment, or absence when prenatal rejection is present.[12] When a mother carries unresolved trauma, it can affect her cortisol levels, her emotional availability, and even her ability to imagine her baby with joy or hope. Children born into these climates often enter life with mistrust, anxiety, or rejection already woven into their identity.

These early wounds often live beneath the surface. They show up later through emotions, dreams, or struggles that seem hard to trace. As Kalsched notes, suffering in early relational contexts can sculpt an "inner world" divided between survival and hope, fear and trust.[13] Trauma leaves profound imprints that shape how we relate to ourselves and to others.

But trauma is not the end of the story. God's love is greater than what has been passed down. His mercy can reach into the past, break cycles of rejection, and write a new legacy of hope. My own journey—through therapy, prayer, and ultimately the writing of this book—has shown me that naming the wound is the first step toward healing it. And healing one generation opens the door for the next.

This book is not only about individual experiences but also about the legacies we carry. It is about breaking cycles and finding language for what was once unspoken. It is for the mothers who did the best they could with what they had. It is for the sons and daughters still trying to make sense of a love they never felt but always needed.

12. Verny and Kelly, Secret Life of the Unborn Child.
13. Kalsched, The Inner World of Trauma, 15.

By telling the truth about what has been passed down, we reclaim the power to write a new ending—not defined by shame, but by restoration. Fraiberg[14] observed, "The baby in these families is burdened by the oppressive past of his parents from the moment he enters the world. The parent, it seems, is condemned to repeat the tragedy of her own childhood with her own baby in terrible and exacting detail." These "ghosts in the nursery" are not mere metaphors; they are psychological truths, passed down through wounds left unhealed.

Research affirms that how a mother was cared for in her infancy becomes a blueprint for how she later cares for others. Bowlby[15] proposed that early attachment experiences form internal working models that guide later parenting. Winnicott[16] likewise emphasized how early relational conditions shape the inner world and capacities beneath awareness.

Yet even this painful awakening can become a sacred invitation. When a mother recognizes her longings and embraces her story with compassion, she creates space to bond differently—with herself and with her baby. Pre- and perinatal psychotherapy offers one pathway for such healing. As mothers confront their legacy, they disrupt the repetition of trauma. What was once unspoken is brought into the light. The unborn child, rather than inheriting silence or shame, can receive something new: presence, safety, and love.

Disparities in the Womb: Race, Stress, and the Cost of Being Born Unwanted

While the wound of being unwanted transcends race, class, and culture, it does not exist in a vacuum. Research has shown that racial and socioeconomic disparities can significantly shape prenatal experiences and maternal health outcomes. Data from the CDC

14. Fraiberg, Adelson, and Shapiro, "Ghosts in the Nursery," 387.
15. Bowlby, *Attachment and Loss: Volume I.*
16. Winnicott, *The Maturational Processes and the Facilitating Environment.*

2022a; CDC 2022b show that Black women in the United States face significantly higher maternal mortality rates than other groups—at 49.5 deaths per 100,000 live births, compared to 19.0 for White women, 16.9 for Hispanic women, and 13.2 for Asian women.[17]

Moreover, disparities persist in prenatal care access and pregnancy-related stress: compared with White women, Black women are much more likely to begin prenatal care late (e.g., in the third trimester) or receive inadequate care altogether. These realities can create emotionally complex prenatal environments—ones that influence not only the mother's well-being but also the emotional climate of the womb.

Such disparities are not solely the result of individual behaviors but are deeply influenced by broader systemic factors: unequal access to healthcare, economic hardship, and a long-standing mistrust of medical institutions within marginalized communities. These layered stressors may intensify the sense of disconnection a child carries into the world—but they do not define the child's worth or destiny.

A child's worth is never determined by their socioeconomic environment or the systemic pressures that may have surrounded their birth. This book affirms the dignity, resilience, and value of every life—especially those born in hard places. The ache of being unwanted may be more visible in some communities due to compounding factors, but the journey toward healing belongs to us all. According to Dominguez,[18] persistent racial discrimination during pregnancy functions as a form of chronic, bodily-wearing stress that contributes to adverse birth outcomes.

This stress affects hormone levels—especially cortisol, which helps regulate how the body responds to pressure. When cortisol is constantly off-balance during pregnancy, it can interfere with how the baby develops in the womb. This may be one way trauma gets passed from one generation to the next—not just emotionally, but biologically.

---

17. CDC, *Maternal Mortality Rates* and *Racial and Ethnic Disparities in Maternal Health*, 2022.

18. Dominguez, "Race, Racism, and Racial Disparities."

When pregnancy is experienced in the context of poverty, housing instability, or racialized medical neglect, the likelihood of emotional disconnection or rejection—conscious or unconscious—may increase. This phenomenon often goes unspoken, especially within communities that have historically lacked safe spaces to process grief, emotional neglect, or trauma related to conception and birth.

Research suggests that Black mothers are more likely to report feeling unseen or dismissed by healthcare providers. This invalidation not only affects the mother's mental health but may also interfere with her ability to bond with the developing child. In my own nonprofit private practice, I have yet to meet a single mother who expressed excitement about her pregnancy.

Most are young, raising multiple children by different fathers, and navigating life with little to no support. Many are homeless, staying in shelters, or caught in the aftermath of broken relationships. These mothers genuinely love their children and often do everything they can to protect them from repeating the same painful path. Yet love alone does not erase the weight of poverty, trauma, and rejection.

Even while loving their babies deeply, many continue to struggle emotionally and practically, leaving unspoken wounds that can echo into the next generation. To fully understand the lived experience of being born unwanted, we must look not only at psychological and familial dynamics but also at the broader sociopolitical realities that shape them. The narratives in this book are not isolated stories; they reveal the complex intersections of personal trauma and structural injustice. Addressing the wound of prenatal rejection, then, requires not only personal healing but also a willingness to confront the systems that make such rejection more likely.

On Gratitude, Redemption, and the Power of Choice

Cortizo[19] highlights how the mother–child bond begins in the womb, underscoring the vital importance of interacting with and caring for the baby from the earliest stages of life. In a similar vein, Sivaraman et al.[20] discuss the ongoing debate over whether these prenatal exchanges are conscious interactions or emerge from nonconscious origins. Whatever the origins, the message remains clear: intentional connection in the womb—whether carried by a single mother, a married couple, or a partner navigating unexpected circumstances—can offer the child greater chances for emotional stability, empowerment, and long-term success.

This book honors that truth while also addressing a difficult but necessary topic. While each participant in this study was the result of an unwanted pregnancy, none believed that abortion should have been the solution. In fact, everyone expressed gratitude that their mothers chose to carry them to term—despite the hardship, shame, or fear surrounding their conception. Their stories are living proof that even when the beginning is marked by prenatal rejection, the ending can still be one of redemption.

This work does not seek to judge the decisions others may make in moments of crisis, but to emphasize this truth: being unwanted in the womb does not mean being unworthy of life. Healing is possible. Purpose is not erased by a painful beginning. And hope belongs to every child—wanted or not.

About the Stories Shared

The stories shared in *The Womb Remembers* are drawn from my doctoral research, which investigated the lived experiences of seven adult participants who self-identified as having been born from unwanted pregnancies. These narratives were originally collected using Interpretative Phenomenological Analysis (IPA), a

19. Cortizo, The Calming Womb Family Therapy Model.
20. Sivaraman et al., "Maternal–Fetal Attachment."

qualitative research method designed to explore personal meaning and lived experience.

Each participant engaged in a one-on-one, semi-structured interview lasting approximately 60–90 minutes, which was transcribed and thematically analyzed. For the purposes of this book, I have also included two additional client narratives (Sarah and Dee) to broaden the conversation and illustrate themes that extend beyond the dissertation data. Alongside these, I weave in my own story, which appears under the name "Naomi."

All names and identifying details have been changed to protect confidentiality, including those of family members. The pseudonyms used here remain consistent with those assigned in my dissertation, with the exception of the two added case studies. While the sample size was small, the richness of these narratives offers invaluable insight into the emotional imprint of prenatal rejection and the long road toward healing. Each account is accompanied by clinical and biblical reflection, with the aim of connecting psychological theory, faith-based truth, and the ongoing search for restoration.

Although no one can consciously recall their time in the womb, participants were able to describe how the knowledge of being unwanted—whether revealed through family narratives, maternal disclosure, or lived experience—had shaped their emotional lives and relationships. Some researchers in the field of prenatal psychology have suggested that traces of these earliest experiences may be stored in implicit memory. In studies using hypnosis and regression, for example, adults have described impressions of being unwanted or rejected even before birth,[21] reinforcing the idea that the womb experience leaves a lasting emotional imprint. Their stories gave voice to the echoes of prenatal rejection: a deep sense of disconnection, struggles with belonging, and questions of identity that lingered long after childhood.

---

21. Verny, *The Secret Life of the Unborn Child*; Chamberlain, *Babies Remember Birth*; Janus, *The Enduring Effects of Prenatal Experience*.

Note to the Reader

Even if we cannot consciously remember the womb, our hearts often carry the unspoken weight of those earliest experiences. Prenatal rejection—even before birth—can leave us questioning our worth, our place in the world, and whether we truly belong. But these hidden wounds are not beyond the reach of healing. God, who formed us in the secret place (Psalm 139:13–16), knows how to meet us even in the places we cannot remember. His love speaks a better word than rejection, reminding us that we were wanted by Him before the foundation of the world.

1

The Beginning Before the Beginning

BEFORE WE ARE HELD, we are carried. Before we are named, we are known. Long before we understand the world around us, we absorb the world within the womb. The idea that the womb experience shapes the emotional and psychological landscape of a person isn't new. Birth psychology—a field pioneered by nurses and clinicians—has long emphasized the profound importance of the prenatal environment on human development. Early observations in hospital nurseries revealed something striking: babies whose mothers were anxious, emotionally distant, or conflicted during pregnancy often seemed unsettled after birth. They cried more easily, were harder to comfort, avoided eye contact, or carried tension in their little bodies. Such tender beginnings remind us that the womb experience leaves its mark long before a child takes their first breath.

For nine months, the womb offers warmth, rhythm, and protection. But the infant receives more than physical nurture—there is also an atmosphere absorbed deep within: was the child anticipated with joy or met with dread? Was there peace surrounding the pregnancy, or turmoil? Acceptance or rejection? These intangible elements soak into the developing life, imprinting messages that may not be spoken aloud but are nonetheless felt. And as the child grows, the essence of who they are begins to surface, carrying traces of those earliest impressions. In this way, the womb is more than a biological shelter; it is the first classroom of belonging—or of fracture.

These observations reinforce the understanding that bonding begins before birth, with the prenatal emotional environment shaping a child's capacity for trust, emotional regulation, and social connection. The attentive care of nursing staff provided some of the earliest evidence that prenatal emotional health matters not only for safe deliveries but also for long-term psychological and relational well-being.[1]

My personal comprehension of this phenomenon deepened in 2010 during my own therapeutic journey, when I encountered terminology that gave voice to a longstanding, unnamed experience: prenatal rejection. The realization that I had been unwanted in utero was profound—not only because it resonated personally but because I recognized a generational pattern. My mother was born unwanted, as was I, and subsequently, my daughter. Three generations of women, each bearing an invisible wound.

That realization marked the beginning of both a personal and professional journey that would later lead to this manuscript. In 2021, I completed my doctoral dissertation, *Giving Voice: An Interpretative Phenomenological Analysis of Those Born from Unwanted Pregnancies.*[2] It was more than an academic pursuit—it was a labor of healing, not just for me, but for the women and men whose stories became the foundation of this book. The participants I interviewed offered more than research data—they offered fragments of their soul. Each one bravely shared the imprint left on their lives by the knowledge—spoken or unspoken—that they were not wanted in the womb.

1. Bibring et al., The Psychoanalytic Study of the Child.
2. Sharp, "Giving Voice."

Rather than measuring outcomes, my research turned toward listening—toward giving space to the voices of those who carried the wound of prenatal rejection. Within these pages, nine stories unfold. Seven arise from the participants of my study; two others were added along the way, one of them my own. Woven together, they speak a shared truth: even the earliest rejection leaves its mark, yet healing is still possible. Some heard the words spoken plainly: *"I didn't want you."* Others discovered it in silence, in absence, or in love that came with conditions. These stories are tender and unguarded, layered with longing, ache, and glimpses of grace.

As I listened, I began to hear not only their pain, but echoes of my own. Their memories revealed the enduring effects of prenatal rejection—a wound that forms before language, before behavior, before choice. Its imprint often surfaces later in life as depression, anxiety, relational struggles, deep insecurity, or a persistent sense of being "too much" or "not enough."

Each story was unique, yet unmistakable patterns emerged. Though the circumstances differed—faces, families, timelines—the internal wounds bore a haunting similarity. Over time, I gathered these common threads into five core themes. They became more than organizing categories; they became mirrors, reflecting the many ways early rejection etches itself into the human heart.

1. *Unwantedness*—The foundational experience of not being celebrated, accepted, or planned. For many, this was the silent starting point—the ache of not being wanted, even in the womb.

2. *Foundational Lies*—Distorted messages absorbed early on: *I'm a mistake. I don't matter. I'm too needy. I'll always be rejected.* Such lies burrowed deep, shaping identity and casting long shadows over future relationships.

3. *Traumatic Life Events*—Physical, emotional, or sexual trauma layered upon that fragile foundation. Each event compounded the ache and reinforced the lies.

4. *Attachments Past and Present*—The continuing impact of insecure or broken bonds with caregivers, partners, and children. Love became something feared, avoided, or anxiously pursued.

5. *Pathways to Healing*—Yet, even in the midst of sorrow, healing began to emerge. Some found relief through therapy, others through faith, and many through both. Each story carried a flicker of hope—a sign that restoration is possible, even after years of pain.

Maternal Bonds and Early Wounds

A common thread woven through these stories is the complicated, often fractured, relationship with the mother. For some, she was emotionally unavailable, overwhelmed, or weighed down by her own unresolved pain. For others, there was outright rejection, abandonment, or silence. Such maternal dynamics laid the groundwork for early attachment disruptions and planted the silent wounds of unwantedness and unworthiness. Naming the mother's role is not about casting blame—it is about recognizing how these earliest connections shape the foundation of identity, belonging, and the ability to receive love.

As life unfolds, those earliest beginnings are often layered with additional complexities—abuse, trauma, neglect, or abandonment. These later wounds can obscure or intensify the original imprint of prenatal rejection, making it difficult to distinguish the root from the fruit. In the therapeutic world, we often differentiate between bonding and attachment. Bonding is immediate and foundational—it reflects a mother's initial love and acceptance of her baby, often beginning during pregnancy. Attachment, by contrast, is the reciprocal relationship that develops over time as needs are met, safety is provided, and trust is formed. According to attachment theory, healthy attachment can still emerge even after a rocky start. Yet without the warmth of early bonding, attachment may carry subtle gaps—hard to name, but deeply felt.

Empirical evidence reinforces that unwanted and unplanned pregnancies are common—and their impacts vary. While often used interchangeably, unintended and unwanted pregnancies are not the same. An unintended pregnancy refers to one unplanned at the time of conception, regardless of emotional response.

An unwanted pregnancy often involves an emotional rejection of the pregnancy itself—and, by extension, the child. It is this rejection, not merely poor timing, that leaves the deepest emotional and spiritual imprint on the child. According to the Guttmacher Institute, between 2012 and 2017 approximately 45% of all U.S. pregnancies were unintended, and among those ending in abortion, about 42–43% were categorized as unwanted.[3] Mental health research shows that individuals who experience an unintended pregnancy may face increased risk of postpartum stress, depression, and anxiety—especially when social or emotional support is lacking.

Yet outcomes are not predetermined. Some children born from unintended or unwanted pregnancies do thrive—often because someone "came along later with love," providing the emotional support needed to rewrite their early story. A thoughtful review by *Verywell Mind* highlights that even so-called "oops babies" can grow into emotionally healthy individuals when met with consistent, nurturing care.[4]

This data reveals three important truths:

1. *The scope of the problem*—Unwanted pregnancy and its emotional consequences touch lives across backgrounds, cultures, and generations.

2. *The presence of risk, not inevitability*—Being born unwanted increases vulnerability to emotional and relational struggles, but it does not dictate destiny. These beginnings may shape the story, but they do not have to define the ending.

3. *The redemptive power of love and care*—Even when love was absent or delayed in the beginning, healing remains possible.

3. Chiu, Maddow-Zimet, and Kost, *Unintended and Unwanted Pregnancy*.
4. Cherry, "Unintended Pregnancies and Their Effects on Children."

With intentional connection, supportive relationships, and grace, restoration can unfold later in life.

Why This Matters

To be unwanted is more than a circumstance. It becomes a message. A message that whispers: *You don't belong. You shouldn't be here.* When that message is absorbed at the most vulnerable stage of life, it does not stay contained in the past. It seeps forward, shaping how we see ourselves, how we love, and how we are loved in return.

But messages can be rewritten. Truth can break through. And wounds can become places where light enters in. This book is for those who have always felt different—for the ones who wrestle with self-worth, who sabotage their own progress, or who carry an unnamed sadness that lingers. It is for the women and men who quietly suspect that their beginning still echoes in their present. It is also for the helpers—for therapists, pastors, parents, and leaders who long to understand this invisible wound and learn how to support the journey of healing.

Rewriting the Story

What if the beginning could be changed? Among clinicians and spiritual caregivers, a conviction is growing: mothers must heal before giving birth—so their children do not have to heal *from them.* The womb is more than biological. It is a spiritual and emotional atmosphere. When it is filled with fear, shame, unresolved trauma, or rejection, the developing child absorbs more than nutrients. They absorb messages.

Messages that whisper

You are a burden.
You are unloved.
You were never meant to be.

Again, this book is not about blaming mothers. It is about breaking cycles—naming how unhealed pain can pass quietly but powerfully from one generation to the next. And it is about hope: that through awareness, compassion, and healing, the story can be rewritten.

The pages ahead weave together stories, psychological insight, and spiritual reflection. You will meet individuals who were unwanted, yes—but also individuals who began to heal. People who found language for their pain. They discovered that rejection could not silence the call of God, which reaches further than human wounds and endures beyond every silence.

A Necessary Distinction

The distinction matters because many of us can recall moments when we felt unwanted—not because love was absent, but because fear or uncertainty took center stage. Womb rejection is different. It is not a fleeting moment but a consistent environment, and its effects echo long after birth.

Reflection

The past is not fixed in stone.
Truth has the power to speak louder than old lies.
Even the deepest wounds can become places where God's presence shines through.
The story you inherited does not have to be the story you pass on.
What began as rejection can be transformed into belonging.
Where pain once lived, healing can begin.

2

What the Soul Carries

OUR BODIES ARE STORYTELLERS. Even when the mind forgets, the
soul remembers—quietly, deeply, without permission. The soul ar-
chives what the mind cannot bear, and the body often becomes its
messenger. We carry within us the whispers of the womb: the tone
of our mother's voice, the rhythm of her heartbeat, the atmosphere
of welcome or worry that surrounded our forming frame. Before
we ever spoke a word, our body had already begun to speak on
our behalf.

Sometimes, that language shows up in ways we do not understand—tension without explanation, anxiety with no traceable
cause, a sadness without a name. It is as if our bodies carried the
residue of rejection long before we understood what it meant to
be rejected.

Science calls it cellular memory—the idea that our bodies
can retain emotional imprints from our earliest experiences, even
before words existed. Scripture calls it being "knit together" in
a womb already known by God. I call it the quiet ache—a soul
memory of not being embraced when it mattered most.

This chapter explores how the soul carries what the heart cannot bear, and how the body reveals what the soul has held in silence—and what it means to gently listen to what both have been trying to say all along.

The Imprint Beneath Awareness

Prenatal experiences are not stored as memories in the traditional sense. A newborn cannot recall with clarity the moment they were formed. But they can reflect it.

That reflection often shows up in subtle ways:

- in how they respond to touch.
- in whether they can be soothed or remain restless.
- in an unexplainable distress when separated from the mother.

In other words, what the child cannot remember with words, the body remembers with reactions. Long before language, the body speaks. Neuroscience calls this *implicit memory*—impressions carried in the nervous system even when the mind cannot recall them. Poets might call it the soul's first language. And when that language is shaped by rejection or unrest, it writes a script the child may carry long into life.

These earliest imprints often form the backdrop of a child's emotional life. They are quiet, invisible, and yet powerful enough to shape how a person feels about belonging, safety, and love. Research in the fields of perinatal psychology and trauma studies has shown that stress hormones like cortisol can cross the placenta. If a mother experiences prolonged anxiety, fear, or depression during pregnancy, the unborn child is often affected physiologically. Their tiny systems adjust to an environment where stress is the norm—setting a baseline for hypervigilance, emotional dysregulation, or even physical ailments later in life.

I know of a woman who spent her entire pregnancy in emotional turmoil—caught in constant conflict with her partner, overwhelmed by fear and instability. Her son is now five. His tender years are already shaped by therapy sessions and medication meant to calm storms he cannot name. His body began bracing for impact long before he entered the world.

But beyond biology, there is something else—a spiritual echo. A child not welcomed may feel the absence of that welcome in ways that defy logic. A baby in the womb exposed to conflict may carry the residue of that turmoil, even without words to name it. A child whose presence was cloaked in shame or secrecy may grow beneath that same shadow, never knowing why.

We call it being "*sensitive.*"

We call it "*needy*" or "*clingy.*"

But sometimes, what we are seeing is grief—the body's grief, carried from the very beginning.

The Story Underneath the Symptoms

In therapy, I've sat with many individuals who don't understand why they feel like a burden in every relationship. They say things like:

- "*I always feel like something bad is about to happen.*"
- "*It's like I'm just waiting for the other shoe to drop.*"
- "*I feel like I don't really fit anywhere.*"
- "*Even when things are good, I can't relax.*"
- "*There's a sadness in me I can't explain.*"

For some, these feelings can be traced to childhood experiences—overt neglect, abuse, or emotional absence. But for others, the sadness predates memory. It lives in the nervous system, in the posture of the heart. It lives in the soul—beneath words, beneath logic, beneath time.

Earlier, I described how our beginnings can leave an imprint beneath awareness. In therapy, I often see how those imprints take shape in the body itself—in what I call the *somatic imprint*—when the body remembers what the mind cannot hold.

Some clients recall their mother saying, *"You were a mistake,"* or *"I wasn't ready for another child."* Others were born into silence—never hearing anything, but somehow absorbing everything. And their bodies responded accordingly: by tightening, shutting down, flinching, or fleeing.

One Client's Story: Sarah (pseudonym)

Presenting Problem: Sarah came into therapy weighed down by persistent sadness that seemed to linger no matter what the circumstances. Her self-doubt colored nearly every decision, leaving her uncertain of her worth and abilities. She described a long history of relational disappointment—patterns of distance, disconnection, and unmet expectations that reinforced her sense of being unloved and unseen. Beneath her words was the quiet ache of unresolved grief and the longing to feel secure in relationships.

Diagnosis: Sarah met the criteria for *Dysthymia (Persistent Depressive Disorder)*—a chronic, low-grade depression marked by a steady presence of sadness and hopelessness. Beyond this, her history suggested elements of unresolved grief and attachment-related trauma, which complicated her mood and contributed to the ongoing difficulties she experienced in sustaining meaningful, trusting connections.

Narrative

Sarah came to therapy at age sixty-five, soft-spoken and reflective, but deeply tired. She sat across from me in the quiet of the counseling room, her hands folded neatly in her lap as though bracing herself. "I think I have a chemical imbalance," she said early on. Her voice didn't shake, but her heart did.

She carried a sadness "for as long as I can remember"—a grief that clung to her very identity. Sarah had two adult sons, a recent divorce from the man she once called "Mr. Wonderful," and a job as an art instructor. From the outside, she seemed stable. But inwardly, she carried a quiet ache.

Her parents had provided a home, food, and education—all the basics. On the surface, her foundational needs were met. But as psychologist Abraham Maslow's hierarchy of needs reminds us, survival is not enough; human beings also require love and belonging.[1] That tier of nurture was absent in Sarah's home. "They weren't very nurturing," she said almost dismissively. I pressed gently. She paused, then looked at me with quiet intensity: "Oh—I forgot to tell you. I was adopted." In that moment, the thread unraveled. Sarah had never named that early separation as trauma, never connected her lifelong sadness to the rupture at the very beginning of her life. But her soul had been carrying the story all along—sadness, disconnection, self-doubt—while her body gave it voice through quiet grief.

As Sarah reflected further, she mentioned her adoptive brother—someone she rarely spoke about. She described him as a "screw up." Though they were raised in the same household, they remained strangers at best, a distance that only reinforced her sense of being different and alone.

Psychological Imprint

Adoption, while often well-intentioned and sometimes necessary, carries an undeniable rupture—a primal separation from the biological mother that can leave a lifelong imprint. For many adoptees, even those raised in stable homes, this early disconnection disrupts the foundation of safety and belonging. The child, long before words, internalizes the message: *I was left behind. I was not chosen.*

For Sarah, outward stability concealed an inner world marked by unresolved grief and fractured identity. Choosing not to connect with her biological family brought a measure of relief, yet it also left questions unanswered. The rupture of adoption cast a long shadow over her perceptions of love, safety, and worth. Beneath

---

1. Maslow, "A Theory of Human Motivation," 370.

the psychology, however, lay something deeper—a spiritual wound that whispered lies about her worth and identity, shaping how she saw herself long before she could put it into words.

Insight as Therapist–Interviewer

As a therapist, I always ask my clients whether they want to include their faith in our sessions. Research continues to show that spirituality can play a vital role in healing—offering meaning, resilience, and a sense of belonging. Still, each client's autonomy must be respected. Some choose to weave their faith into the process; others do not. When I asked Sarah, she was clear that she did not want to bring faith into her therapy, and I honored that choice. Her story is told in the same way—without a spiritual overlay—because respecting her choice was itself a step toward creating safety and trust.

I was both Sarah's therapist and her interviewer, which gave me a unique window into her lived experience. In the therapy room, labels were never enough; what Sarah needed most was to be deeply seen and heard. That became clear the day she spoke the words almost in passing: *"I was adopted."*

She offered the words casually, as though they were an insignificant detail. To her, it did not seem to matter. Yet as we explored together, I sensed their hidden weight. What Sarah dismissed as unimportant revealed itself to be a quiet key—explaining why sadness lingered, why trust was fragile, and why she often felt like a stranger in her own story.

Ironically, around the same time I met Sarah, I had begun watching a television program where adoptees were searching for or reconnecting with the families who had given them away. Each episode carried stories of longing, loss, and unexpected redemption. I could not help but notice the timing. Here I was, listening to Sarah's story of adoption, while watching countless others unfold on the screen before me. It felt like more than coincidence—it felt like preparation, as though God were weaving together what I was seeing and hearing so I could better understand the ache of beginnings.

Though Sarah did not believe her adoption was central to her identity, she was fascinated by the insights surrounding prenatal rejection. She leaned in when we spoke of how unwantedness or separation in the womb could echo long after birth. That curiosity was itself a doorway—an opening toward understanding and, eventually, healing.

Her decision not to reconnect with her biological family revealed the protective boundaries she had built around her deepest wounds. Therapy offered Sarah the safety to bring her story into the open, and the interview provided a frame to name and acknowledge it—two experiences that, together, moved her closer to healing.

Naming her adoption was not the end of the story; it was the threshold. In that moment, even without embracing its full significance, she stepped closer to truth—not to be crushed by it, but to begin reclaiming what had been lost in the silence of early separation.

Spiritual Insight

On a spiritual level, rejection strikes at the core of identity. A child who enters the world unloved, or whose arrival is met with ambivalence, becomes vulnerable to destructive messages. Psychology may call this the *inner critic*—the harsh inner voice that distorts truth and fuels shame. Scripture names the source of those lies *the enemy of our souls.* Both point to the same reality: distortions that fracture belonging and sow insecurity.

Lies that say: *You were a mistake. You are forgettable. You are alone.* But rejection is not the final word. Scripture speaks a greater truth: that every life is intentional, fearfully and wonderfully made, seen by God before the first breath.

Though Sarah's story carries the mark of human rejection, it is overshadowed by divine welcome. Adoption may tell part of her journey, but the larger narrative is one of belonging and love written by the Creator Himself.

Note from the Father's Heart

My dear one,

I have watched you carry a weight you were never meant to bear. I have seen your sorrow, your questions, and the ache that lingers in silence. I know the years of loneliness that made you wonder if love was ever truly meant for you. I know how disappointment has marked your steps and how shame has whispered that you are not enough.

And still—I call you to Myself. Even when others withheld love, I was reaching toward you. Even when you felt unseen, My eyes never left you. You have never been forgotten in My presence.

I am not asking you to strive or perform. I am calling you to rest. To come as you are, without fear of being turned away. My love for you is steady, not fragile; eternal, not fleeting. I am not ashamed of your questions, nor afraid of your pain. Bring them all to Me, and you will find that I am nearer than you ever imagined.

In My presence, you will find the gentleness your soul has longed for and the love that will never let you go. Let Me speak a new word over you—not rejected, but welcomed; not abandoned, but embraced; not invisible, but fully seen and delighted in.

I am calling you home to My heart. Come, rest in My love. You are Mine, and nothing will ever change that.

—Jesus

Hope Woven Into the Frame

But here is the beauty: just as the soul carries the wound, the soul can also carry the healing. Through therapy, spiritual renewal, and gentle attention to both body and soul, many begin to feel safe within themselves for the first time. Breathwork, trauma-informed counseling, prayer, and the simple presence of compassion help bring regulation where there was once chaos.

The body that braced for rejection can soften. The heart that carried shame can rest in dignity. And the soul that remembered pain can now remember peace.

Healing takes time. And it rarely begins with answers, but with awareness. Sometimes the very details we dismiss as unimportant—like Sarah minimizing her adoption—are the ones holding the invitation to healing. What we call small, God may call significant.

Pause and consider:

- Are there pieces of your own story you have brushed aside?
- Memories you rarely speak of because they seem insignificant—or too painful to name?
- Could those hidden pieces hold both the wound *and* the key to healing?

Hope does not deny the wound. It reframes it. And in that reframing, what once was carried as grief can slowly become carried as grace.

Follow-Up

Sarah continues to engage in therapy and has slowly begun to identify the emotional patterns shaped by her early adoption. As a child, she was told by her adoptive parents that her birth mother was very young when she placed her up for adoption. Though intended as a gentle explanation, Sarah internalized it as evidence that she was never truly wanted, and this belief shaped the emotional climate of her childhood. Confronting this painful reality has been a difficult but necessary step in her healing journey.

Since then, she has begun creating art not only as an instructor but also as a personal form of expression and restoration. She is still learning how to receive love without suspicion, yet she now sees herself with greater kindness and compassion.

Reflective Questions

1. Have you ever felt a deep sadness that seemed to have no clear starting point?

2. In what ways has the absence of nurturing or emotional attunement shaped your relationships?

3. How do you tend to respond when love feels distant or conditional?

4. What would healing look like if it began with acknowledging the grief you were never allowed to express?

3

A Crack in the Foundation

AT FIRST, SOME CRACKS are invisible. They form beneath the surface of a story, small shifts that remain unseen until something sacred begins to break. In human lives, these fractures often emerge in the hidden core of identity.

This chapter traces how early wounds in bonding and emotional attunement leave marks on the foundation of self-worth. Parenting styles and attachment patterns—two powerful shapers of the soul—carry the ability to either strengthen or weaken the sense of belonging we were created to know.

Parenting Styles

Parenting styles shape more than rules; they create the emotional atmosphere in which a child learns who they are, how they are loved, and what is expected of them. Psychologist Diana Baumrind identified four key styles:[1]

---

1. Baumrind, "Effects of Authoritative Parental Control," 890; Baumrind, "Current Patterns of Parental Authority," 15.

- *Authoritative*: High warmth, high expectations. These parents are responsive, nurturing, and set clear boundaries. Children raised in this environment tend to develop secure attachments and healthy self-esteem.

- *Authoritarian*: Low warmth, high expectations. Rules are enforced rigidly, with little emotional support. Children may obey but often feel unseen or unloved.

- *Permissive*: High warmth, low expectations. These parents are indulgent and avoid setting limits. Children may feel adored but lack guidance and structure.

- *Neglectful/Uninvolved*: Low warmth, low expectations. Emotional and physical needs may be ignored altogether. These children often experience profound insecurity and confusion about their value.

Attachment Styles

Attachment refers to the emotional bond formed between a child and their primary caregiver, which becomes the template for how they relate to others throughout life. Attachment theory, pioneered by John Bowlby and expanded by Mary Ainsworth, outlines four primary styles of emotional bonding:[2]

- *Secure Attachment*: The child feels safe and consistently cared for, which fosters confidence and healthy relationships.

- *Avoidant Attachment*: Emotional needs are frequently dismissed. The child learns to self-soothe by detaching.

- *Anxious Attachment*: Care is inconsistent. The child becomes hypervigilant, clinging or overly sensitive to abandonment.

- *Disorganized Attachment*: The caregiver is a source of both comfort and fear. This confusion often leads to internal chaos.

2. Bowlby, *Attachment and Loss*, Vol. 1; Ainsworth et al., *Patterns of Attachment*.

Each of these styles leaves a distinct emotional residue. And when a child is born unwanted—or simply uncared for in a meaningful way—these foundational cracks deepen.

One Client's Story: Nicole (pseudonym)

Presenting Problem: Nicole presents with long-standing sadness and depression, struggles with low self-worth, and a history of unhealthy coping, including alcohol use and relational instability. She reports insomnia, chronic anxiety, and unresolved trauma stemming from sexual violation, the wound of adoption, abortion, and family instability.

Diagnosis: Nicole meets the criteria for Major Depressive Disorder, recurrent and moderate to severe, marked by sadness, hopelessness, and persistent low self-worth. In addition, she carries a diagnosis of Generalized Anxiety Disorder, Alcohol Use Disorder in sustained remission, and Post-Traumatic Stress Disorder (PTSD). She also demonstrates attachment-related concerns consistent with an anxious attachment style.

Narrative

Nicole agreed to meet with me, carrying both curiosity and surprise that such a study was being conducted. She admitted she had never heard of research that sought to give voice to those born from unwanted pregnancies, and the thought that her own story might matter beyond her private struggles moved her deeply.

Nicole's childhood was shaped by both provision and fracture. Her adoptive parents were hardworking and educated, but their marriage was fragile and eventually ended in divorce. Praise was rare. Comfort was distant. Even as a child, she sensed something was "off." At age eight, she was told she had been adopted—a revelation that only confirmed what she had always felt: that something about her belonging was uncertain, conditional.

From that uncertainty, perfectionism took root. Nicole excelled in school, not because she felt secure, but because she believed achievement might cover the ache. "I knew I was smart," she recalled, "but I was always sad. I always knew something wasn't quite right." Her drive carried her into a demanding career as an ER doctor, but even there, the wound of rejection followed.

In relationships, she over-functioned. She poured out more than she received. The same striving that made her excel in medicine left her vulnerable to burnout, broken partnerships, and a persistent sense of aloneness. Her history carried deep violations: sexually assaulted while on a date, one abortion, and repeated encounters with rejection. To numb the ache, she turned to alcohol in college, a habit that followed her into adulthood and led to several run-ins with the law. Her nervous system never fully settled. Insomnia, depression, and anxiety became her steady companions.

She poured herself into performing for love, carrying the deep belief that simply being herself was never enough. Even when she met her birth mother and siblings years later, the fracture remained. The connection never grew, and the belonging she longed for continued to slip through her grasp.

Nicole's story, however, does not end in despair. She eventually sought therapy—first on her own, and later with her daughter, who also wrestled with feelings of low self-worth. For the first time, she stepped into a space where she didn't have to perform, where her story was safe, and where her value was no longer measured by achievement. Little by little, she began to loosen the grip of alcohol and release the lie that love must be earned.

Her journey shows that anxious attachment often traces back to the earliest fractures—sometimes even in the womb, where life is granted but welcome is withheld. When belonging feels fragile, a child learns to strive for love. Healing begins, however, when the striving gives way to rest and the soul embraces the truth that has always been present: you are loved, you are wanted, you are enough.

Psychological Insight

Children raised in unstable homes often internalize a fragile sense of worth. When love feels conditional—offered or withheld depending on performance, behavior, or circumstances—a child learns that belonging must be earned. Their value becomes tethered to achievement, obedience, or the avoidance of failure.

When paired with anxious attachment, this dynamic intensifies. The child becomes hypervigilant—constantly scanning for signs of approval or rejection. This heightened sensitivity serves as survival, but it comes at a cost: chronic anxiety, emotional exhaustion, and a nervous system that never fully rests.

For Nicole, the imprint was present from the very beginning. She was adopted by a professional couple whose marriage was unstable and eventually dissolved. Affirmation was seldom offered, and comfort was kept at a distance. Even before she knew she was adopted, she carried an unspoken sense of disconnection—a fracture in belonging that left her with questions she could never quite articulate.

Uncertainty left Nicole chasing a sense of worth she could never quite grasp. Success came easily, but satisfaction did not. Even as she built a demanding career in emergency medicine, the quiet ache of rejection remained.

At the root was a belief she could never shake: love had to be earned. That conviction propelled her forward but also left her weary, vulnerable, and ashamed. When the ache grew too heavy, she reached for alcohol to quiet it—a relief that never lasted. The weight of unresolved trauma and numbing patterns deepened the wound, carving traces across both body and soul.

Insight as Therapist-Interviewer

While I was not Nicole's therapist, my role as interviewer allowed me to glimpse her inner world. What became clear was this: Nicole didn't need mending—she needed a place to rest. She needed a safe space where achievement did not define her worth and where love was not measured by performance.

Beneath the layers of accomplishment and anxiety was a little girl still longing to hear: *You're already enough.* Healing for Nicole did not come through striving harder, but through unlearning the lie that her worth was earned. Therapy created space for her story to breathe—for truth to slowly replace shame.

Spiritual Insight

Rejection leaves more than memories; it etches itself onto the soul. For Nicole, adoption was not merely a fact—it was an ache that whispered, *You were not worth keeping.* Shame crept into that silence, twisting truth into lies: *You must prove yourself. You must earn love. You must hide your sorrow.*

So she pressed on.

She poured herself into the classroom.

She drove herself in the emergency room.

She worked relentlessly to prove she was enough.

She gave everything she had in every relationship, hoping relentless effort would soothe the silent ache within. But then God's voice broke through the striving: *You are Mine. You are chosen. You are loved—not because of what you do, but because of who I Am.* Nicole wrestled with belonging, caught between worlds and unsure where she fit. God didn't meet her with explanations or accolades but with the promise of His presence: *I will be with you.* Her healing came not through striving but through surrender; not through applause but through the quiet assurance of being seen, known, and loved by the One who never leaves.

Note from the Father's Heart

My beloved daughter,

You were never a mistake. Long before others decided what to do with your life, I had already written your name in My heart.

Though people may have failed to hold you in the way you longed for, I have held you from the beginning. I know the ache of being passed from one set of arms to another, the questions that have haunted you about your worth, the fear that no one would truly stay. I have seen how rejection has whispered lies—You are not wanted. You are not enough. Those words did not come from Me.

I am calling you to Myself. You do not need to perform for My love or prove that you are worthy of belonging. In My eyes, you already belong. Let Me quiet the striving. Let Me still the anxious wondering. Rest in the truth that you are chosen—not as an after-thought, but as My delight.

The void left by human failure can be filled with My presence. I am the Father who does not abandon. I am the One who gathers the lonely and places them in families. Where others may have turned away, I turn toward you with joy.

So come close, My daughter. Let Me hold the places that still feel fragile. Let Me breathe life where grief has lingered. You are Mine— not by accident, not by force, but by love. And nothing in all creation will ever separate you from that love.

—Jesus

Hope Woven Into the Frame

When identity is fractured, healing requires more than changing behavior. It calls for a deep rewiring of belief—moving from conditional worth to unconditional love. Nicole's story reminds us that healing begins not in striving, but in resting; not in achieving, but in receiving. Foundations do crack. But cracks can be mended, and light can shine through the places once broken.

The God who rebuilds ruins (Isaiah 61:4) is also the One who restores the soul (Psalm 23:3). Where shame once wrote its verdict, grace now writes a new name. Healing is not the absence of scars but the presence of hope. In Christ, even fractured identities find wholeness—and the pieces we thought too shattered to matter become part of His radiant mosaic.

Follow-Up

Nicole remains in therapy, now joined by her daughter. Together they are learning a new way of being—one where worth is not measured by perfection, but by presence. Nicole no longer consumes alcohol and has begun to repair some of the relationships fractured by shame and striving. The healing journey continues, but it no longer begins with achievement. For Nicole, it begins with truth.

Reflective Questions

1. Do you ever feel pressure to achieve or perform in order to be accepted?

2. When did you first learn that being "good" or "successful" made you feel more worthy of love?

3. How has unpredictability in early caregiving shaped the way you relate to others?

4. What might it look like to rest in the truth that your value is not in what you do, but in who you are?

4

Chosen In Spite of It All

SOME BEGINNINGS ARE QUIET—NOT because nothing was said, but because nothing was celebrated. To be born unwanted is not just an unfortunate circumstance; it is an emotional wound that begins before memory and extends far beyond the moment of birth. It is the ache of a child who enters the world already carrying the burden of rejection. No balloons. No welcome. Just a hush that speaks louder than words.

For some, this silence lingers only in the background, barely noticed until life's disappointments bring it to the surface. For others, it becomes the defining undertone of their entire story, shaping how they see themselves and how they relate to the world around them. This hidden wound often shows up as sadness without explanation, striving without satisfaction, or loneliness even in a crowded room. It is here that we meet Chantel.

One Client's Story: Chantel (pseudonym)

Presenting Problem: Chantel entered therapy carrying the weight of low self-worth that shaped how she saw herself and how she related to others. She struggled to trust in relationships, often fearing abandonment or betrayal, which left her isolated and unsure of where she belonged. Her history included unresolved trauma that continued to resurface in her thoughts and behaviors, along with episodes of self-injurious behavior that revealed the depth of her inner pain and her struggle to cope.

Diagnosis: Chantel met the criteria for Persistent Depressive Disorder (Dysthymia), reflected in her ongoing sadness and lack of hope. She also exhibited features of Complex PTSD, rooted in prolonged relational and developmental trauma. Alongside these, Chantel showed clear signs of Identity Disturbance—difficulty establishing a stable sense of who she was, apart from the wounds and rejection she had carried for years.

Narrative

For Chantel, the silence began at a bus stop. Her mother was waiting—waiting to end the pregnancy—when God intervened. Out of nowhere, a stranger approached and handed her a pamphlet that read: *"Don't do it. God has need of you."* Those words pierced through her fear and confusion. In that moment, everything shifted. She turned around, went home, and chose to carry the baby to term.

But though she chose life, the seed of rejection had already been sown. Chantel's mother didn't want to be pregnant. She was in a toxic relationship and grappling with her own unresolved pain and unmet emotional needs.

For nine months, Chantel's forming soul absorbed an atmosphere of unwantedness—no songs of joy, no words of celebration, only silence heavy with rejection. Such beginnings leave their own imprint long before a child takes her first breath.

However, Chantel's mother loved her the moment she laid eyes on her. Still, love alone does not always undo the imprint of prenatal rejection—especially when those roots run deep across generations. The longing to be wanted begins before birth, and when that need is unmet, even a mother's genuine love at first sight may not fully silence the echoes of earlier rejection. Later in life, her mother confessed that she, too, had been unwanted. And her mother before her. The pattern was unspoken but painfully present. What had not been healed had been handed down.

From an early age, Chantel sensed something was off. She was musically gifted—her voice beautiful, her heart tender—yet she carried a sadness that seemed older than she was. In childhood, she was molested by a female cousin, an experience that deepened her feelings of unworthiness. She longed for a relationship with the father she barely knew, but the absence only reinforced her ache. Over time, she began to resent the woman who gave her life, seeing herself less as a beloved daughter and more as a burden.

Unwantedness is not always shouted. Sometimes, it is whispered in sighs, in the absence of touch, in hurried glances and unmet eyes. The child, though unable to articulate it, absorbs it. This kind of rejection imprints not just on the heart but on the nervous system. It becomes a lens through which the child views themselves—and the world.

Research confirms what many therapists have long sensed: early emotional environments matter. Children born into rejection—even if clothed and fed—often internalize a deep, lingering question: *Was I ever truly welcome here?* And when that question goes unanswered, a silent struggle begins.

When Chantel entered therapy, she was worn out from life. Years of striving, searching, and merely surviving had left her depleted. On the surface, her struggles looked like anxiety and depression. But as her story unfolded, it became clear that beneath those symptoms lay deeper wounds: the pain of being nearly aborted, the weight of generational rejection, and the rupture of entering the world from a place of reluctance.

In time, her pain spilled over into her body and her choices. She became a frequent patient on psychiatric wards across different hospitals. Cutting became her way of releasing what she could not put into words. More than once, she even pulled the trigger, intending to end her life—only to find the barrel jam each time.

These moments, though dark and terrifying, revealed something hidden: even in her most desperate attempts to escape, her life was being preserved. What could have ended in silence became another marker of survival—a sign that her story was not finished, and that God's hand was present even in the places she thought He had abandoned her.

It was in this context that Chantel later recalled a conversation with her mother: *"You weren't planned. I wasn't ready. But God told me to keep you."* At first, those words gave her hope—until she realized that being kept was not the same as being wanted. That distinction pierced her, confirming why she carried such a heavy sense of rejection beneath the surface.

Her story is not unique. Children who enter life without a sense of being wanted often grow up balancing gratitude for life with grief over the absence of welcome. For Chantel, this tension explained the love–hate relationship she carried toward her mother. Scriptures like Psalm 27:10 speak of God's unwavering embrace even when parental love fails. But Chantel didn't yet experience Him that way; for much of her life, she saw Him as a hard taskmaster rather than a refuge.

Over time, her mother made attempts to "right her wrongs," to soften the distance that had been present from the beginning. But for Chantel, the damage had already been done. The ache of early rejection could not simply be undone by later gestures—it had to be faced, named, and healed.

Psychological Insight

The ache of rejection, left unnamed, will always find a way to speak. For Chantel, it spoke through her body, her relationships, and her restless pursuit of belonging. Though her basic needs had been met, her soul carried an invisible hunger.

Her emotional development was shaped by an early environment steeped in unresolved pain, volatility, and inconsistent nurture. Trauma and rejection—especially in those earliest years—do not just shape thoughts; they shape identity. Chantel wrestled with a fractured sense of self—tender yet angry, gifted yet restless, longing for love yet afraid of being truly seen.

Her same-sex attraction and revolving door of toxic relationships were not simply about orientation or choices. They were expressions of her deep search for safe attachment—for someone who would stay. When early bonds are unstable, adulthood often carries their echo. The ache resurfaces, not always recognizable, but always familiar.

The scars on Chantel's body told the story her words could not. Self-injurious behaviors (cutting) became both a cry and a release. Multiple hospitalizations revealed the depth of her despair. And though she pulled the trigger more than once in an attempt to end her life, the gun jammed every time. Psychologically, these behaviors revealed a nervous system overwhelmed by rejection, dysregulated by trauma, and struggling to anchor itself. Yet they also bore witness to something else—that survival, against all odds, was still part of her story.

Insight as Therapist-Interviewer

As I listened to Chantel's story, I realized she had been marked by God. Long before she could understand it, He was weaving preservation into her life. That bus stop encounter was not just her mother's turning point—it was also the moment God claimed Chantel's future.

That awareness reshaped how I heard everything Chantel shared. The hospital stays, the scars on her body, even the failed suicide attempts—they were not just signs of despair, but signs of preservation. Again and again, God was saying: *You are Mine. Your story is not over.* Chantel's struggle with identity and rejection was real, but so was the mark of God's intention over her life. What she needed was not another voice telling her who she wasn't, but the steady reminder of who she already was: chosen, loved, and preserved for purpose.

Spiritual Insight

Survival, against all odds, was not accidental—it was evidence of divine preservation. Where rejection had tried to define her, God was still writing a different story. Spiritually, rejection is one of the adversary's most destructive strategies. He doesn't always shout—sometimes silence is enough. The silence of Chantel's beginnings left a door open for self-hatred and confusion. Though her life had been spared again and again, the adversary sought to convince her that her life carried no value.

But rejection does not have the final word. The same rejection that scarred Chantel's identity became the very place God began to reveal His unconditional love. *"He heals the brokenhearted and binds up their wounds"* (Ps. 147:3). *"For I know the plans I have for you. . ."* (Jer. 29:11). And Jesus Himself, who was *"despised and rejected by men"* (Isa. 53:3), shows us that rejection is not the end—it is the soil where God restores identity, purpose, and belonging.

Chantel knew how to recognize God's voice, but she didn't yet have a personal relationship with Him. She grew up attending church and would occasionally return as an adult, but her faith remained more familiar than intimate. She could sense Him speaking—even in moments when she was "running the streets"—yet pain often spoke louder.

Though God's hand was evident in the earliest chapters of her life, Chantel struggled to see Him as a loving Father. For much of her journey, He seemed distant and demanding—more like a taskmaster than a refuge. The seeds of divine purpose were there from the beginning, but they lay buried beneath years of pain and misunderstanding.

Chantel didn't want to be the chosen one, yet God had already spoken: "Before I formed you in the womb, I knew you. Before you were born, I set you apart" (Jer. 1:5). Being chosen doesn't shield you from rejection; it means that even in rejection, God continues to call your name.

Note from the Father's Heart

Beloved Daughter,

I saw your mother that day at the bus stop. She thought she was alone, but I was with her—and I was with you. In the hush of that moment, I watched the weariness in her eyes, the weight pressing on her shoulders, and the questions she couldn't bring herself to speak. I also saw the small life tucked beneath her heart—the one no one had named yet. I knew you then, before you ever had words to whisper back.

I chose you in that quiet—not because you were flawless or easy to love, but because you were always meant for more than a beginning defined by fear. My choosing is not about perfection; it is about purpose. Even when you cannot feel it, My pattern of care is being woven around you—one that no human absence can undo.

When you pushed Me away, I did not turn from you. When you felt too far gone, I moved closer. I meet you in the places that hurt the most: where shame has settled, where loneliness lingers, where silence has been loudest. I do not wait for you to earn My presence; I am already there—steady, sure, and unchanging.

And every time you have walked through the doors of My house, I have whispered the same truth over you: "You are Mine. You belong to Me. Nothing can separate you from My love." I have repeated it again and again, not because you have not heard, but because I want it to sink deeper than the lies that once shaped your heart.

You are not the shadow of someone else's sorrow. You are not a mistake to be hidden. You are the living proof of mercy arriving when all seemed lost. Come near: bring Me the places you've been taught to hide. Breathe in My acceptance. Let the soft counter-song of My love replace the hush that marked your beginning.

Your story is still being written. The stanza that began in silence will not be the final line. You are wanted. You are named. You are Mine—cherished, held, and being formed for the good things I have prepared for you.

—Jesus

Hope Woven Into the Frame

Rejection doesn't always come with words. Sometimes it slips in quietly—in the long pause of a mother's sigh, in shoulders that stiffen instead of soften, in the silence where songs of joy should have been. It can take root in atmosphere as much as in action, leaving a forming soul to wonder about its welcome before its first breath is drawn.

And yet, the story doesn't end there. Just as rejection can begin before birth, so can healing. Healing stirs when awareness dawns—when we dare to name the ache we've carried without language, when we let truth touch what silence once covered. It begins when we loosen our grip on striving and open our hands to receive love as the gift it has always been.

To be wanted by God is not a consolation prize—it is the deepest belonging. To be chosen by Him means you are seen when others overlooked you, known when others misunderstood you, and loved even when human love faltered. From that foundation, hope takes root. And from that place—where truth speaks louder than pain—the story begins to change.

Follow-Up

Chantel continues to engage in therapy, slowly unpacking the layers of generational pain and rejection she once buried under rage and rebellion. She has begun to embrace the idea that her worth is not determined by others' ability to love her, but by God's decision to preserve her life—even before she was born.

Today, Chantel no longer identifies with the cycle of toxic or same-sex relationships that once marked her search for connection. Her healing journey has led her to embrace a deeper sense of identity and worth, rooted not in past wounds but in the love of God—a love she now believes she was chosen for all along.

Trust remains a challenge, but her heart is softening. Music, once an escape, has become a sacred space of connection and healing. And she is beginning to see that the One who saved her at the bus stop never stopped calling her chosen.

Reflective Questions

1. What messages—spoken or unspoken—did you receive about your worth in early life?

2. When did you first sense you were unwanted, or that love came with conditions?

3. In what ways has that early imprint shaped how you relate to others today?

4. What would it mean to believe, deeply, that your life was not a mistake?

5

The Lies We Lived

BEFORE WE EVER SPEAK a word, we begin telling ourselves stories—about who we are, what we're worth, and whether we belong. These stories do not always come from truth. Many are born from pain. They form quietly, shaped by our earliest experiences of being seen or overlooked, accepted or abandoned.

Long before we form conscious thoughts, we absorb impressions:

A mother's tension during pregnancy.

A father's absence.

A household filled with criticism or silence.

The feeling that your very presence is an inconvenience.

Over time, these impressions take root as beliefs:

I don't matter.

My voice doesn't count.

I'm always the problem.

They are not always spoken aloud, but they are lived. Lived in the way we apologize for existing. In the way we stay silent to keep the peace. In the way we push ourselves to achieve, hoping to earn the love we never felt we deserved. These are the lies we lived—and sometimes still live—until healing invites us to live from truth.

The Foundation of False Identity

From the earliest moments of life, children make sense of the world in simple, self-centered ways. Not out of pride, but because the developing mind hasn't yet learned to separate *self* from *circumstance*. As Jean Piaget described, this is *cognitive egocentrism*—the natural tendency for a child to believe, *If something is happening, it must be because of me.*

So when a parent is distant, angry, or emotionally unavailable, the child doesn't wonder, *What's wrong with them?* Instead, they quietly conclude, *Something must be wrong with me.* Add the deeper wound of being born unwanted, and the message grows louder: *I was never supposed to be here.*

Over time, these impressions don't remain fleeting thoughts. They harden into identity. They become the scaffolding on which self-perception is built, whispering lies that follow into adulthood: *You're too much. You're not enough. You were never meant to be.* These aren't small insecurities—they are foundational lies that fracture identity, distort relationships, stifle purpose, and feed shame.

Research in attachment and developmental psychology confirms this: the messages we absorb from our earliest caregivers shape not only how we see ourselves, but how we engage with others and the world. When those early messages are tainted by rejection or inconsistency, they become woven into our inner dialogue—often without us even realizing it.

Cognitive Behavioral Therapy (CBT) seeks to identify and reframe these distorted beliefs. But true healing often requires more than reframing—it requires returning to the original wound and allowing a deeper truth to rewrite the narrative. This chapter begins to explore what it costs to live under those lies—and what it takes to confront them with truth, even after years of quiet agreement.

One Client's Story: Joshua (pseudonym)

Presenting Problem: Joshua entered therapy burdened by a cycle of shame, anger, and harsh self-criticism. His persistent negative self-talk reinforced the belief that he was flawed and unworthy, fueling both emotional volatility and withdrawal from others. These struggles often surfaced in his relationships, where he vacillated between longing for acceptance and anticipating rejection.

Diagnosis: Joshua met the criteria for Persistent Depressive Disorder (Dysthymia), evidenced by chronic sadness, irritability, and diminished hope for the future. Clinical consideration was also given to Complex PTSD, as his history suggested features of trauma-related symptoms, including hypervigilance, intrusive memories, and relational distrust.

Narrative

Joshua, now in his forties, carried a quiet rage. During our work together, he shared that from as early as he could remember, his mother referred to him as a *"bastard."* The word struck him like a whip—sharp, humiliating, unrelenting. "Words hit just as hard as fists," he once said, recounting not only the insults but also the absence of affirmation.

He wasn't told he mattered. He was told, implicitly and explicitly, that he was a burden.

His earliest memories were filled with comparisons to his siblings, cruel nicknames, and scorn. Over time, he began to see himself through the eyes of others—through a cracked lens. Unlovable. Unworthy. In the way.

In adolescence, Joshua found himself in yet another argument with his mother. But this time, her words cut deeper than anything he had heard before: *"I should've never had you! But I gave birth to you, didn't I? What more do you want?"* In that instant, whatever illusion of safety remained was gone.

Those words lodged themselves in his soul. It wasn't just anger—it was confirmation of what he had long suspected: that his presence was tolerated, not treasured. That sentence settled like cement over his heart. When Joshua sat across from me, his body often spoke louder than his words—shoulders slumped, eyes lowered, a faint flinch whenever kindness was offered. It was as if love itself were a language he had never learned. He didn't simply wonder if he was hard to love; he carried the deep belief that he was defective.

Those early wounds seeped into his adult life. Though married for several years and raising two children with his wife, the relationship bore the weight of his past. He also had a teenage son from a previous relationship—a child he hardly knew—leaving that bond fragile and uncertain.

The ache of rejection shaped the way he related to those closest to him. His hunger for affirmation sometimes drove him into choices that only deepened his shame, including an affair that carved mistrust into his marriage. Yet even in failure and consequence, Joshua held onto his faith. He often said that trusting God in the middle of the mess was the only thread keeping him from unraveling completely.

Through our interview, Joshua began to see that the convictions he carried were not unshakable truths but stories—narratives born of pain, reinforced by rejection, and repeated until they felt permanent. But stories can change. What shame had written, truth could rewrite.

Psychological Insight

Joshua's emotional landscape reflects the long-term impact of chronic verbal abuse and early rejection. Being called derogatory names during childhood—especially by a primary caregiver—is a form of emotional maltreatment that can deeply shape a child's developing self-concept. Over time, those words became not just insults but internalized beliefs about who he was.

CBT teaches that thoughts, feelings, and behaviors are closely linked. Joshua's recurring thoughts—*I'm defective. I don't belong. I'm unlovable.*—produced persistent emotional pain and led to avoidance in his relationships. These are examples of cognitive distortions, thought patterns that often take root in childhood and then reinforce themselves over time.

His story also reflects a struggle with identity formation, a conflict central to Erik Erikson, a German-born American psychoanalyst known for his theory of psychosocial development. In Erikson's fifth stage—*Identity vs. Role Confusion* (adolescence)—the task is to develop a stable sense of self.[1] Identity formation is the process of answering life's most basic questions: Who am I? Am I wanted? Do I belong? Erik Erikson described it as the central work of adolescence, yet its roots are planted much earlier. A child who grows up surrounded by love and affirmation carries those messages forward into a stable sense of self. But when affirmation is absent—or when a child is born unwanted—identity formation is disrupted.

Instead of developing a secure identity, the individual often carries fragmentation into adulthood, marked by instability, self-doubt, and chronic shame. For Joshua, this disruption was compounded by the reality that he was unwanted from the beginning. Long before he had words, rejection had become part of his foundation. Later, the names he was called as a boy only reinforced what had already been sown in silence—that his very existence was questioned. Those early and later messages together became the lens through which he saw himself as a man.

Reflection

Rejection is never a single wound. Left unhealed, it multiplies into two silent companions: self-rejection and fear of rejection. Self-rejection turns the pain inward, whispering lies like, *"I am not enough. I am unworthy."*

Fear of rejection turns the pain outward, bracing for abandonment even when love is present. Together, they create a cycle of striving and hiding—shaping how we see ourselves and how we

---

1. Erikson, *Identity*, 128–35.

relate to others. But rejection is not the final word. Healing begins when the lie is named and God's truth speaks louder than the echo of rejection.

Insight as Therapist-Interviewer

Though I was not Joshua's clinical therapist, my role as interviewer gave me a window into the depth of his wounds. What became clear was that Joshua had never been given the chance to mourn the rejection he carried. Rather than grieving it, he had absorbed the wound, allowing it to shape who he believed himself to be. Over time, those false messages became the framework of his life—lies he lived as though they were truth.

Our conversations became a process of peeling back those lies—naming them for what they were: distortions, not destiny. Joshua's question wasn't clinical; it was deeply human. *"Do you think someone like me can be loved—really loved?"* he asked, almost in a whisper. I didn't respond with theory. I answered with what he most needed to hear:

"Yes, Joshua. You are already loved—loved by God before you ever took your first breath. Not because of what you do, but because of who you are. But now it's time to fall out of agreement with the lies you've carried and step into the truth. Not just any truth—the truth of God's Word spoken over your life: that you are chosen, seen, and cherished."

That moment did not erase the years of pain, but it marked a turning point. It was the first crack in the armor of falsehood—the beginning of Joshua's realization that love had always been possible, and that his worth was never in question.

Spiritual Insight

Rejection is more than an emotional wound; it leaves an imprint on the soul. What psychology names the *inner critic,* Scripture calls the *accuser*—the voice that twists pain into lies. These lies often disguise themselves as personality: *I'm just quiet. I prefer to be alone. I don't need anyone.* Yet beneath them often lies a hidden fear: *I don't want to be hurt again.*

For Joshua, that narrative began before birth. Prenatal rejection planted the seed, and years of shame watered it until he wore it like armor. He *was* unwanted—and he knew it. But what began as a painful reality slowly settled into his sense of self. *Unwanted* was no longer just what happened to him; it became who he believed himself to be. The accuser's whispers hardened into identity-shaping accusations: *You're a mistake. You don't belong. You're too much. You're not enough.*

This is the true danger of early rejection—it distorts self-perception until even God's presence feels distant. Over time, the lies spoke louder than love. But God was not silent. *"Can a mother forget the baby at her breast and have no compassion on the child she has borne? Though she may forget, I will not forget you"* (Isa. 49:15).

Joshua's life was never an accident—it was divinely authored. Healing began when the false narrative was exposed and confronted with truth. The story he had been handed was not the one God had written.

Note from the Father's Heart

My child,

Before a single star was hung and before the earth knew its name, I knew yours. You were not a mistake. I formed you in secret and breathed life into you because you were mine by design.

When the world turned away, I did not. When hands pushed and words cut, I stayed. When a silence settled where welcome should have been, I listened, and I wept with you in the quiet places no one else could see.

You have been told many things about yourself—lies worn like armor, truths denied like sunlight. I did not write those lies. They were spoken by wounded people, spoken by fear, or slipped in by the whisperer who would have you live small. But hear me now: those words do not define you.

You are chosen. You are beloved. You are not the byproduct of someone else's sorrow but the living proof of mercy and grace. Your worth is not measured by achievement, approval, or the applause of others. It is measured by My steadfast love—unchanging, unearned, wide as the sky.

I do not call you to pretend the hurt didn't happen. Bring your anger. Bring your sadness. Bring the questions that keep you awake. Let them be spoken. Let them be held. Grief is not failure; it is a doorway to healing. I meet you there, not to shame what you carry but to walk with you through it.

If you have been living by the voice that says you must earn love, it is time to stop agreeing with that lie. Step with me into the truth I speak over you. Let My Word rewrite the story that fear has been telling. I will be the steady pulse beneath your doubt, the quiet yes beneath your no.

Come closer. Rest in the arms that will not withdraw. Receive the mercy that arrives when the world is silent. You are wanted. You are called. You are mine—and I will not let the story end in shame.

With an unending, tender love,
Your Father

Hope Woven Into the Frame

I've sat across from adults who carry themselves like ghosts—present, but not fully alive. Their hearts still echo the words no child should ever hear: *"You're a mistake." "You're not wanted." "You're a problem."*

These aren't just painful words. They are identity wounds. And they don't fade with time. They must be met with truth—gentle truth, bold truth—the kind that does not dismiss pain, but rewrites the story it tried to tell. Even in Scripture, we see this pattern: those born into hardship or rejection often become carriers of God's redemption.

- Joseph—betrayed by brothers, sold into slavery, yet raised up to save nations in famine.

- Moses—hidden as an infant, raised in Pharaoh's house, yet chosen to deliver Israel from bondage.

- David—overlooked as a shepherd boy, yet anointed king of Israel.

And yet—each was seen. Each was chosen. Each was called. So it is with us.

Follow-Up

Joshua's journey has not been easy, but it has been honest. Since naming the lies he once believed—that he was a mistake, a burden, and illegitimate—he has begun the work of rewriting his identity.

He is actively confronting the shame that once ruled him and is learning to speak more gently to himself. While trust still comes slowly, he has committed to staying present and grounded, especially in relationships that once triggered his deepest insecurities. Slowly, he is learning what it means to be known without fear.

Reflective Questions

1. Have you ever absorbed a lie about yourself that shaped your identity?

2. How do you tend to respond to rejection or criticism—both internally and outwardly?

3. What truths from Scripture, or from your own faith tradition, speak directly to those lies?

4. What would it look like to shed false labels and begin reclaiming your true identity?

6

When Healing Finds Its Voice

THERE IS SOMETHING SACRED about telling the truth—not only the facts of our lives, but the feelings that were buried beneath them. For those who carry trauma, finding words can feel like walking through a minefield. Silence becomes a survival strategy, a way to endure the unspeakable. But silence can also become a prison. Healing begins when we risk breaking that silence. When the unspoken finally finds language, the weight begins to lift.

Speaking our truth requires vulnerability—an act of bravery that is both terrifying and freeing. It is a declaration that our story matters, that our pain is real, and that we are worthy of being heard and understood. Yet this process is rarely neat or linear. Healing is often messy, cyclical, and deeply personal.

In this chapter, we meet Dee—a woman whose pain had long gone unnamed. Her story is not tied with a ribbon, nor is it a straight line. But in finding the courage to speak, she began to discover the courage to heal.

Her journey reminds us that healing does not require perfection, nor does it demand that we hold all the answers. It begins with telling—sharing the stories we have kept locked away, the truths that have shaped us, and the hopes that still flicker beneath the surface.

May Dee's story invite you to consider your own: What stories remain untold within you? What truths are waiting to be voiced? And what kind of healing might unfold when you dare to share your heart, even in its brokenness?

One Client's Story: Dee (pseudonym)

Presenting Problem: Dee came to counseling overwhelmed by emotional instability that often felt beyond her control. She had a history of recurrent psychiatric hospitalizations following episodes of self-harm and suicidal ideation. Her relationships were marked by cycles of intense closeness followed by conflict and rupture, leaving her isolated and fearful of abandonment.

Diagnosis: Dee met the criteria for Borderline Personality Disorder (BPD), characterized by instability in mood, self-image, and relationships, as well as impulsivity and recurrent self-destructive behaviors. She also carried a diagnosis of Post-Traumatic Stress Disorder (PTSD), stemming from repeated traumatic experiences that left her with intrusive memories, heightened reactivity, and deep emotional scars.

Narrative

Dee was born from an unwanted pregnancy—a truth she would not discover until her teenage years, when her mother hurled it at her in a heated argument. Though spoken in anger, the words pierced her soul and confirmed what she had always sensed but could never explain: her presence was a burden, not a joy.

Even before she could put it into words, Dee carried the weight of being unwanted. Raised by her grandmother, she grew up with the silent imprint of rejection woven into her identity. That unspoken ache, layered with other early traumas, became the root of her fractured sense of self.

By the age of fourteen, Dee had already entered the mental health system, beginning a long cycle of psychiatric hospitalizations that would stretch into adulthood. By her early thirties, she was a single mother to a young son, yet her days were marked by rage, abandonment, and a profound emptiness that seemed impossible to fill.

Her history bore the weight of unspeakable trauma. As a child, Dee witnessed her brother shoot and kill their father during a violent family altercation. That moment shattered what little sense of safety she had left and became the unspoken core of her emotional dysregulation.

Dee's life unfolded in ruptures—trauma upon trauma. There was the betrayal she felt during inpatient stays, when she hoped for care but instead felt dismissed. There was the shame she carried over her struggles with cannabis use. There were the unstable and toxic relationships, especially with her child's father, that left her feeling even more deeply abandoned. Each wound pressed the same conclusion deeper into her soul: she was unsafe, unwanted, and unworthy of lasting connection.

Her symptoms reflected classic patterns of borderline personality disorder: volatile emotions, an intense fear of abandonment, unstable relationships, and a fragile sense of self that always seemed on the edge of shattering. In therapy, Dee wavered between craving closeness and recoiling from it. On some days she leaned in with warmth and hope; on others, even the gentlest guidance felt threatening.

This back-and-forth was not manipulation—it was survival. It was her nervous system's way of testing what her heart most longed to know: *Is this space truly safe? Will you stay if I show you how broken I really am?*

Psychological Insight

Borderline Personality Disorder (BPD) is one of the most complex and often misunderstood diagnoses. It is marked by intense emotional dysregulation, unstable relationships, and a fragile sense of identity. For Dee, these were not just symptoms—they were the echoes of a childhood steeped in neglect, rejection, and trauma. Never feeling wanted, truly seen, or safe disrupted her ability to form a secure sense of self. Instead, she lived in a painful in-be-tween—clinging desperately to the hope that someone might finally stay, while bracing for the abandonment she had come to believe was inevitable.

Her story illustrates the profound connection between early attachment wounds and emotional regulation. For Dee, the wound began even before birth. She was conceived unwanted, a reality spoken over her later in adolescence but carried in her body long before she had words for it. That prenatal rejection left its imprint on her developing sense of self, shaping how she experienced safety, belonging, and love.

For individuals like Dee, the brain's threat-detection sys-tems often remain on high alert, triggering overwhelming fear responses at even the slightest hint of rejection. What others see as instability is, in truth, the body and soul's attempt to guard against the pain of being unwanted all over again. These patterns are not moral failures or character flaws—they are adaptations to unre-lenting pain and loss.

Recognizing this truth is the first step toward compassion and healing. Dee's journey underscores the need for trauma-informed care that looks beyond behavior to the wounds beneath it. True healing requires more than symptom management; it requires safety, trust, and the grace-filled space to rewrite the story that began in rejection but is not destined to end there.

Insight as Therapist–Interviewer

I was both Dee's therapist and her interviewer, determined to help her see that she was more than her diagnosis—that she didn't have to wear it like a cloak. Dee was well acquainted with psychological terminology, Dialectical Behavior Therapy (DBT) skills, and every facet of her mental health journey. She also confessed that Jesus was important to her, often weaving her faith into our sessions.

Some days she welcomed me warmly; other days she ignored my calls altogether. At one point she looked at me and said, *"I thought you would be the one to take away my sorrow."* My heart wept for her. Though I could not erase her pain, hearing her story gave me a window into her deep longing for connection, even beneath the walls she had so carefully built.

Her journey was anything but easy. Trust did not come quickly. She often wrestled with whether love could truly hold the full weight of her brokenness. But with time, gentleness, and trauma-informed support, small cracks began to appear in those walls. Dee started naming her grief aloud. She stopped apologizing for her emotions. She allowed silence to shift from threatening to sacred.

And, perhaps most significantly, she found the courage to tell her story—not a polished or sanitized version, but the raw truth: that she had been unwanted, wounded, and yet still longed to believe she was worthy of wholeness. That moment became a turning point. Healing began when Dee gave voice to the pain that had once been unspeakable—when she let the words rise, allowed the tears to flow, and finally said, *"I don't want to be this broken anymore."*

Spiritual Insight

Dee's story brought to mind the woman with the issue of blood from Mark 5:25–34—desperate, weary, and uncertain if healing was even possible for her. Like that woman, Dee had traversed a long and exhausting path of treatments, relationships, and interventions. Each one promised relief, but each left her still unseen, still untouched, still unchanged at the deepest level.

What she craved was not fleeting pity or surface-level fixes. She longed to be truly known, deeply loved, and embraced as a beloved daughter of God. From the womb she had carried the unspoken message of rejection, and for much of her life she lived in its shadow. Yet the very ache of being unwanted pointed to her deeper longing—to be received, welcomed, and chosen.

When Jesus spoke the words, *"Daughter, your faith has healed you. Go in peace and be freed from your suffering"* (Mark 5:34), it was more than physical restoration—it was the restoration of identity and worth. For Dee, that same invitation stood before her: the possibility of allowing her fractured story to be met by unwavering love. A moment where shame would no longer have the final word. A moment when the God who sees whispered to her soul, *"You are enough. You are wanted. You are Mine."*

This passage reminds us that healing is never just about symptom relief. It is about reclaiming the dignity, belonging, and identity that trauma tried to steal. For Dee, God's love offered what the world never could—a foundation strong enough for transformation. No matter how shattered the past, in Him there remains hope for restoration.

Note from the Father's Heart

Beloved,

You were never a mistake. Long before time began, I saw you. I formed you. I breathed life into you—not because others chose you, but because I did. The pain you've carried, the silence you've endured, the longing that has haunted your nights—I know it all. I have been with you in every moment.

I am not intimidated by your sorrow or your story. I am the One who gathers your tears in a bottle and calls you by name. Though others may have turned away, I never have. And I never will.

You are not too much. You are not too broken. You are not forgotten. You are Mine. I see the places where shame has written its lie, and I will not let that lie have the final word. I am calling you—not to perform, but to come and rest; not to prove, but to receive.

Bring me the parts you have hidden. Bring me the grief, the anger, the questions. Lay them down. I will meet you there with gentleness. I will breathe peace where there has been turmoil and plant worth where you have been told you have none.

There is a new name I long to speak over you: beloved, chosen, forgiven, delight. Take this truth and let it seep into the places that

once felt hollow. Walk slowly. Healing is patient work, but I am faithful in every step.
    You are Mine—now and forever. Rest in that. Rest in Me.
    —Jesus

Hope Woven Into the Frame

Dee's journey shows us that even the deepest wounds can be touched by hope. Her life was marked by ruptures—by the ache of being unwanted and by the chaos of emotions that felt impossible to manage. Yet in naming her pain, she began to loosen the grip of shame.

The very cracks that once threatened to undo her have become the openings where grace seeps in. Hope for Dee is not the denial of her broken places but the presence of God within them. Her voice, once silenced by fear and rage, is learning a new song—a song of resilience, courage, and belonging. Her story reminds us that hope is rarely neat or linear. It is woven, thread by thread, into the frame of a life that has known sorrow. And in God's hands, even what began in rejection can end in love.

Follow-Up

Dee's life remains challenging, but the small victories matter. Since bravely confronting the trauma of witnessing her father's murder and connecting it with the earlier wound of being unwanted in the womb, she has begun to stabilize. She has established a safety plan she actively uses when triggered, and her psychiatric hospitalizations have decreased significantly. Most importantly, she is learning to tell her story with less rage and more clarity.

Years later, Dee confessed to me that in the beginning she wasn't ready to hear my voice, though she saw that my heart was for her. With time, she came to embrace what I had long wanted her to know—that she was more than her diagnosis. Today, she no longer wears the cloak of Borderline Personality Disorder as her identity.

Instead, she is choosing to embrace who God is and what has already been accomplished for her at the Cross.

Her progress has been steady and real. She no longer smokes cannabis, she has secured stable housing and employment, her relationship with her brother—recently released from prison—is beginning to mend, and her bond with her only son is blooming in new ways. Dee's healing journey is ongoing, but for the first time, she truly believes peace is possible.

Reflective Questions

1. What part of your story have you kept hidden because you feared being misunderstood?

2. What emotions rise within you when you imagine naming that pain out loud?

3. Who in your life has earned the right to hear your story safely and without judgment?

4. What might healing begin to look like if telling your story became the first step?

7

Attachments and Empty Arms

PSYCHOLOGISTS OFTEN DESCRIBE THE first three years of life as critical for emotional development. But what if the attachment wound begins even earlier—before a baby ever takes its first breath? Prenatal psychology reminds us that the womb is more than a biological space; it is the first emotional environment a child will ever know. In that hidden place, trust begins to take root through the rhythm of the mother's heartbeat, the cadence of her breath and voice, and the hormonal "weather" that surrounds the developing child. These steady cues form the earliest sense of safety—a kind of *felt security* registered by the nervous system long before words or conscious memories exist.

When a mother is emotionally detached, conflicted, or weighed down by her own trauma, that stress imprints itself on the developing child. And when that child grows up without consistent nurture—whether through abandonment, foster care, or unstable caregiving—the wound deepens. It becomes a loss that precedes language, yet lingers in the body, heart, and mind.

This kind of rupture is not always visible on the outside. Many children raised in homes that meet their basic needs still carry an ache they cannot name. The absence of consistent love and belonging leaves what some psychologists call an "attachment void"—a hollow place that longs to be filled, often in ways that bring more pain than comfort. Elizabeth's life embodies this ache.

One Client's Story: Elizabeth (pseudonym)

Presenting Problem: Elizabeth came into therapy carrying the heavy weight of severe abandonment wounds that reached back to her earliest years. Her sense of identity was fractured, shaped by maternal rejection and reinforced through cycles of unstable and often destructive relationships.

Diagnosis: Elizabeth met the criteria for Complex Post-Traumatic Stress Disorder (C-PTSD), a condition that develops from prolonged exposure to repeated relational trauma. Her symptoms included intrusive memories, hypervigilance, emotional dysregulation, and deep distrust of others.

Narrative

When Elizabeth first shared her story, she held it with a quiet blend of sorrow and strength. Oldest of six yet never feeling she belonged, her early years were marked by abandonment, instability, and a wound she didn't have words for. At the age of nine, she found the words—not in a whisper but in a shout. Her mother said it in the open, and she said it often: "I didn't want this pregnancy." Each time it landed like a verdict.

Elizabeth learned to survive by becoming useful—second mother, the one who kept the little ones fed, settled, and out of trouble. She wasn't an honor-roll student; school was simply a place to keep her head down. At home she read faces like weather, scanning for storms and shifting herself to keep the peace. Her surprising brightness became both gift and guardrail, a small light she carried so the ache of unwantedness wouldn't swallow her whole.

Only much later would she learn to name the wound—prenatal rejection—and to seek something deeper than managing everyone else's needs: a steadier place, a foundation of inner security, acceptance, and belonging. Even so, Elizabeth's temperament was one of jubilee. She carried a natural lightness, a joy others noticed even in childhood. But behind her laughter lived unspoken questions and unhealed wounds; the joy she offered often masked the ache within.

Her mother battled serious mental illness and was hospitalized on several occasions. She married multiple times, and with each shift in the household, Elizabeth's world grew more unstable. Affection was rare. More often there were insults—cutting words that pierced as deeply as the silence. The one she longed for most felt unreachable, emotionally absent even when physically present.

Eventually, Elizabeth was removed from her family and spent much of her childhood in foster care and group homes. The separation only deepened the wound. She remembered hiding in closets, whispering questions no child should have to carry: *"Why doesn't my mom love me? Why does she hate me so much?"*

The rejection did not fade with time. Elizabeth recalled her mother and other relatives repeating cruel words: *"You weren't supposed to be born. You were a mistake."* Those sentences burrowed deep, convincing her she was unworthy of love—even from the one who gave her life.

And yet, another voice spoke too. Elizabeth remembered knowing the voice of God from an early age—a whisper of presence that cut through the chaos around her. His nearness stood in stark contrast to her mother's absence.

As she grew older, Elizabeth's search for love was careful but desperate. Her relationships were few, but often unstable. She married not out of mutual wholeness, but out of need—the hope that someone would finally choose her. But instead of healing her emptiness, marriage magnified it.

By the age of twenty-eight, Elizabeth had given birth to seven children. Her arms were full, but they never truly felt healed.

Alongside those births were several abortions, each one layering grief upon grief.

One pregnancy in particular still weighed on her heart. She once lay on an abortion table, ready to end her pregnancy, but at the last moment she changed her mind. That son was born—but his life would become marked by turbulence. He carried his own wounds from trauma, and Elizabeth often reflected that perhaps he had absorbed her ambivalence before he ever took his first breath. Though she loved him deeply, their relationship became one of her greatest challenges, shaped by the shadows of prenatal rejection.

And yet, despite her lack, Elizabeth loved her children fiercely. She poured into them from an empty cup, determined they would never feel the abandonment she had carried all her life. As an adult, Elizabeth recalled a moment in church when a pastor prayed over her: *"The Lord says He's bringing you out of Lo-debar."* She later learned that *Lo-debar*, mentioned in Scripture, was a barren place where the forgotten and broken were left to survive. For Elizabeth, those words pierced her spirit. They spoke of God's intention not only to bring her out of the desolation of rejection, but also to restore her identity, dignity, and place at His table.

Psychological Insight

Elizabeth's story illustrates how early rejection and instability do more than cause painful memories—they shape how the brain and body carry life forward. Her difficulty trusting love and her tendency to anticipate abandonment were not signs of weakness, but natural imprints of her earliest environment.

Research on attachment confirms this reality: when a child is not consistently received with joy and safety, the nervous system adapts for survival. Elizabeth's anxiety, her emotional highs and lows, and her deep longing to be wanted were all rooted in this survival wiring.

These imprints often resurface in adulthood, especially in close relationships. Elizabeth's struggles were not random—they were the echoes of her earliest experiences, showing up in the present until she could face them with compassion and truth.

Insight as Therapist-Interviewer

Listening to Elizabeth's story was like hearing lament and praise woven together. Her history bore the marks of prenatal rejection—insults that crushed her spirit, separations that fractured her sense of belonging, and choices shaped by both grief and regret. Yet alongside the pain was a temperament of jubilee and an early sensitivity to God's voice that revealed a resilience trauma could not fully erase.

Elizabeth's search for love was not reckless; it was purposeful—born from the ache of a child longing to be chosen. Her marriage and relationships were less about indulgence and more about survival, an attempt to quiet the relentless echo of *"You were a mistake."* What stood out most was how her mother's instability left her carrying an emotional inheritance she never asked for. And yet, even in retelling her pain, Elizabeth spoke with a surprising strength. Though she often poured from an empty cup, she poured with intention.

It became clear that her healing would not come from rewriting the past but from reframing her story. The prophetic word spoken over her—God bringing her out of *Lo-debar*—was more than spiritual encouragement; it was a reorientation of her identity. It named her story not as one abandoned but as one remembered.

Elizabeth didn't need to be fixed; she needed to be reminded. Reminded that her life was not an accident. Reminded that God had been speaking over her from the very beginning. Reminded that the same God who called her out of barren places would continue to restore her identity and heal the ache of empty arms.

Spiritual Insight

Rejection is more than a painful memory; it seeps into the soul and leaves a spiritual imprint. For Elizabeth, that wound was planted early and reinforced by the voices around her. Words like *"You were a mistake"* echoed louder than lullabies. In place of security, she inherited instability. In place of blessing, she absorbed curses.

Scripture reminds us that "death and life are in the power of the tongue" (Proverbs 18:21). The repeated insults she received became the language of her inner world—convincing her that she was unloved, unwanted, and undeserving of belonging. This is how rejection works spiritually: it distorts truth, twists identity, and makes the lie feel more real than God's promise.

Yet even in those early years, Elizabeth was not without hope. She sought comfort in the Lord Jesus, whose gentle whisper stood in stark contrast to her mother's absence. Though she wrestled with shame and instability, God kept leaving traces of His presence—reminders that she was seen and not forgotten. That is why the prophecy she later received about being brought out of *Lo-debar* carried such weight: it named the barren, forgotten emotional landscape she had lived in for so long, and declared God's intention to restore it.

Elizabeth's life reminds us that being rejected by people does not mean being rejected by God. Where her mother's words tore down, God's Word built up. Where the world said *"mistake,"* God said *"chosen."* And where her arms once felt empty, His presence promised to fill them with the love she had always longed for.

Note from the Father's Heart

My beloved daughter,

You were never a mistake. Before your mother's words, before the rejection, before the shame—you were already Mine. I formed you with intention, and I breathed joy into your spirit. That jubilee you carried, even in the darkest places, was My gift to you—a sign that the light could never be extinguished.

I saw every moment you hid in closets, asking why you were not loved. I heard every insult, every word that told you that you should not have been born. Those were lies, not truth. The truth is this: I chose you. I called you. I have loved you with an everlasting love.

You have given much out of your lack, pouring yourself into your children even when your arms felt empty. I honor the love you showed, even through pain. What you thought was too little, I will multiply. What felt broken, I will redeem.

And now hear this: I am bringing you out of Lo-debar—out of the barren places, out of shame, out of the rejection that tried to bury you. I am calling you to the table, not as a guest, but as My daughter. You belong here—with Me. You are remembered. You are restored. You are loved.

—Jesus

Hope Woven Into the Frame

Elizabeth's story does not end with rejection. While the wounds left their mark, they also opened a doorway for God's redeeming love to enter. What she once believed was a permanent sentence—that she was unlovable, unworthy, unwanted—began to be rewritten as she encountered the One who had always chosen her.

Hope, for Elizabeth, was not about erasing the past but re-framing it. Each scar became a place for grace to rest, each ache an invitation to deeper healing. Her frame—once fragile and frayed—was being rewoven with threads of belonging and worth. And so it is with us. The wounds we carry are not the end of the story. In the hands of the God who heals, even our broken beginnings can become places where hope is stitched into the fabric of our lives.

Follow-Up

Elizabeth is doing well and no longer lives in *Lo-debar.* The barren place that once defined her story has given way to restoration. Her children are thriving, though the son she once considered aborting continues to face challenges. Still, Elizabeth trusts God to bring him out in the same way He brought her out—redeeming what once seemed beyond repair.

Her life today bears fruit she once never imagined. She is now a grandmother, rejoicing in the next generation. She has earned her degree as a chaplain, turning her pain into purpose by ministering to others. Her marriage, once strained by instability, has grown stronger, marked by grace and mutual respect. Above all, her love for Jesus Christ has become her never-ending song of gratitude—a melody that rises from the very places where silence and sorrow once lived.

Reflective Questions

1. When have you felt disconnected from those who were supposed to love and protect you?

2. In what ways have early attachment wounds shaped or influenced your adult relationships?

3. Are there places in your life where you still feel "given away" emotionally or unseen?

4. What would safe, secure connection look like for you in this season of your life?

8

The Search for a Safe Place

BEFORE WE SEARCH FOR purpose, we search for safety. The human soul is wired to seek shelter—emotionally, physically, spiritually. Safety is not a luxury; it is foundational. As Maslow's hierarchy of needs reminds us, safety sits just above food and water. Without it, love, belonging, and growth remain out of reach.

For George, however, safety was never given. He grew up without a father's protection and with a mother whose words cut deeper than comfort. Instead of shelter, he found instability. Instead of affirmation, he heard insults. Instead of nurture, he endured violation. His earliest experiences taught him a harsh lesson: the world was not safe, and neither was he.

George longed for a place where he could rest, where he would be accepted, where he would finally be enough. That longing followed him through childhood, adolescence, and adulthood. It shaped the way he viewed himself, the way he related to others, and the way he pursued love. "Throughout my life, I have been looking for love," he admitted. Beneath that confession lay a quieter, more painful truth: "No matter what I did, I never felt like I was good enough."

This chapter explores George's story—marked by abandonment, violation, and despair, yet also by glimpses of refuge and redemption. His journey reminds us that the search for safety is not ultimately about circumstances but about presence. Real safety begins when we are seen, known, and still loved.

One Client's Story: George (pseudonym)

Presenting Problem: George came to therapy burdened by deep abandonment wounds and a lifelong struggle with identity confusion. He grew up under the shadow of maternal rejection—his mother often reminding him that his presence had "ruined her life."

Diagnosis: George met the criteria for Complex Post-Traumatic Stress Disorder (C-PTSD), marked by intrusive memories, emotional dysregulation, hypervigilance, and chronic difficulties with trust and intimacy. He also presented with features of Major Depressive Disorder, including persistent sadness, hopelessness, and periods of withdrawal.

Narrative

George carried himself with a quiet heaviness. It was as if life had pressed down on his shoulders for far too long. He had never known his father. His mother, burdened by her own struggles, made little effort to hide her resentment toward motherhood. "*I never wanted kids,*" she admitted in her angrier moments. George later described her as a "*party girl,*" more interested in her own freedom than in raising children. When anger flared, she lashed out at her sons with words that cut deep and lingered: "*You guys ruined my life.*"

Instead of affirmation, George received insults. Instead of nurture, he endured emotional and verbal abuse. But the betrayal ran deeper still. When he was young, his mother often sent him to a neighbor's house for babysitting. What she did not see—or would not acknowledge—was that the adult man there violated him. The experience was devastating. George learned early that his body was not safe and that trust could collapse into danger in an instant.

With no father to protect him, no mother to affirm him, and no safe place to speak of what had happened, George carried the wound in silence. Shame grew roots, convincing him that he was unwanted, unworthy, and alone. "No matter what I did," he later reflected, "I never felt like I was good enough."

As he grew older, that unspoken pain fractured his sense of self. Without affirmation, he doubted his worth. Without protection, he became wary of intimacy and fearful of rejection. His despair deepened further when his brother died by suicide—a devastating loss that reinforced George's belief that life was fragile, unbearable, and sometimes not worth living.

By seventeen, George's story began to shift. He found work with a local family who welcomed him as their own. For the first time, he experienced consistent kindness and encouragement. When his mother eventually kicked him out, this family opened their home to him. Their love became a refuge—a glimpse of what family was meant to be.

That bond deepened over time, and George eventually married the daughter of the family who had first hired him. Though marriage brought its own challenges, it anchored him to the first real experience of acceptance and stability he had ever known.

Even so, the shadows of his past never fully disappeared. George carried forward the boy who had once hidden in silence, still longing to hear the words neither parent ever spoke: *You matter. I'm proud of you. You are mine.*

His story circled back to the confession he voiced from the beginning: "Throughout my life, I have been looking for love." That longing defined his childhood, shaped his adolescence, and followed him into adulthood. And yet, even in the places where love was absent, George's journey bears witness to a deeper truth: the ache itself points to the kind of love we were created for—a love that never fails.

Psychological Insight

George's experience demonstrates how unwantedness, emotional neglect, and early violations can significantly disrupt the process of healthy identity formation. From the beginning, he carried the unspoken message that his life was a mistake. His mother admitted she never wanted children and often lashed out with words like, *"You ruined my life."* For George, rejection began in the womb, and those words only reinforced what he already sensed: he was not wanted.

Developmental psychologist Erik Erikson taught that identity is first shaped through belonging, describing the earliest stage of psychosocial development as *Trust vs. Mistrust.* When caregivers are responsive, a child learns that the world is safe and that they are worth caring for. When caregivers are detached, resentful, or rejecting, the child internalizes the opposite message: *The world is unsafe. I am unworthy of love.*

The insults George heard grew into cognitive distortions—negative core beliefs that shaped his inner narrative: *I am a burden. I ruin things. I am never good enough.* According to Cognitive Behavioral Therapy (CBT), such beliefs do not remain static; they grow into filters through which all of life is interpreted. For George, this meant that even kindness often felt suspect, and belonging felt temporary.

The sexual violation he endured as a child compounded this imprint. Trauma researchers emphasize that childhood sexual abuse fragments identity, layering secrecy and shame on top of already fragile foundations. George's silence was not only about fear but about the absence of a safe and affirming space to speak his truth.

And yet, his story also demonstrates the power of redemptive affirmation. At seventeen, George encountered a family who welcomed him as their own. Their acceptance did not erase the wound of being unwanted, but it gave him his first taste of belonging. It was a corrective emotional experience—one that whispered a different truth: *You are not a mistake. You are worthy of love.*

Still, the tension lingered. George carried two voices within him: one whispering he was never enough, and another reminding him that belonging was possible. His work was learning to let the voice of truth grow stronger than the voice of shame.

Insight as Therapist–Interviewer

Listening to George's story felt like being invited into a lifelong search—a search for affirmation, belonging, and safety that had eluded him from the very beginning. Though I was not his clinical therapist, my role as interviewer gave me a sacred window into both the depth of his wounds and the resilience he carried.

What struck me most was George's honesty. He did not minimize his pain or excuse the harm done to him. He spoke openly of his mother's words—*"You ruined my life"*—and of the abuse he endured at the hands of someone who should have protected him. His body language, his words, even his silence revealed the weight of living as though "unwanted" was his name.

And yet, I also witnessed the quiet strength of a man who refused to give up on love. His voice softened when he described the family who welcomed him as a teenager. His eyes lit with gratitude when he spoke of the men's group that became a place of accountability and healing. These glimpses reminded me that George's life was not defined by rejection alone—it was also marked by resilience, by the pursuit of something better, by a heart that still believed in the possibility of love.

George admitted he still struggles with his thoughts and emotions toward his mother. Forgiveness is not a straight path, and his pain still rises in waves. But he is determined to live life without restraint—to no longer let shame, anger, or rejection dictate his choices. This determination reveals the fruit of his healing: not perfection, but persistence; not a finished story, but a redeemed direction. The work before George was not about fixing what was broken, but about reclaiming what was true. He was never a mistake. He was never too much or not enough. Beneath the shame and silence was a son longing to be named—beloved, chosen, received.

Spiritual Insight

Rejection is never just an emotional scar; it is also a spiritual assault. The adversary of the soul seizes early wounds and twists them into lies that sound like truth: *You ruined everything. You are unworthy. You will never be enough.* For George, those words came first from his mother, then from the silence of abandonment, and eventually from the echo chambers of his own mind.

Rejection wounds twice—first in the words that are spoken, and then in the beliefs that take root. George carried shame like a second skin, mistaking it for identity. What began as painful words eventually became the lens through which he saw himself.

Yet traces of God's love kept breaking through. The kindness of the family who welcomed him as a teenager, and later the strength he found among brothers in a men's group, became turning points in his story. In these spaces, the lies that had shaped his identity began to loosen their grip. Slowly, George came to understand that the love he had spent a lifetime chasing could neither be earned nor lost—it had always been his in Christ.

Scripture affirms this: *"Though my father and mother forsake me, the Lord will receive me"* (Psalm 27:10). For a man who never knew his father and was wounded by his mother, these words became more than verses—they became a lifeline.

As George's love for Christ deepened, God ceased to be a distant figure and became the Father who had never abandoned him. In Christ, George found the affirmation he had always longed for: *You are Mine. You belong. You are enough.* The men's group gave him community, but God's presence gave him identity. What the enemy twisted for shame, God rewrote for redemption.

Note from the Father's Heart

My son,

I was there before your first breath. Even when others said you ruined their lives, I was speaking a different word: You are My delight. You were never a mistake—never unwanted in My eyes. I saw the shame you carried, the silence you hid behind, the weight of words that cut too deep. I grieved with you when trust was broken and when love felt out of reach.

But I also preserved you—through the kindness of strangers, through the embrace of a family who welcomed you, through the brotherhood you found among men who seek Me. Hear Me now: You are not bound by your mother's wounds or by your past.

You are bound to Me. You are chosen, beloved, and received. Do not be afraid to live with your whole heart. Do not let anger or shame keep you restrained. For I am the One who heals your soul, restores your dignity, and gives you a place at My table. You are enough—not because of what you do, but because you are Mine.

—Jesus

Hope Woven Into the Frame

Healing does not erase the past, but it can rewrite its meaning. George's life bears witness to this truth. He may still feel the sting of his mother's words and the weight of childhood violation, but he is no longer defined by them. Where rejection once wrote his identity, redemption is now inscribing a new story.

Hope, for George, is not the denial of pain. It is the courage to live without restraint, to believe that his life is more than his wounds. It is discovering that love was never truly out of reach—it had been waiting all along in the heart of God.

And this is the invitation for us all: what rejection once declared, God now rewrites with belonging. What shame once whispered, grace now answers with truth. In His hands, every wound can become a witness, and every broken story a frame for hope.

Follow-Up

Today, George continues to walk with Christ and remains faithful in his men's group, where he finds both accountability and belonging. While he still wrestles with thoughts and emotions toward his mother, he is committed to forgiveness as a journey and no longer allows bitterness to define him. He is determined to live freely—without the restraints of shame or rejection.

His marriage to the daughter of the family who first welcomed him as a teenager stands as a testimony of grace. What began as rescue has become covenant, a reminder that love can take root even in the soil of broken beginnings.

Though the shadows of the past still rise at times, George's love for Christ and his steady pursuit of healing anchor him in hope. His story reminds us that healing is not about forgetting the pain but about learning to live beyond it—grounded in a love that never lets go.

Reflective Questions

1. Have you ever believed the lie that you were "not enough"? Where did that belief first take root, and how has it shown up in your life?

2. In what ways have words spoken over you—whether affirming or wounding—shaped your sense of worth? Whose voice have you allowed to be the loudest?

3. How have you searched for safety—through people, performance, or escape—and what has that search revealed about your deepest needs?

4. What would it look like for you to live without restraint—grounded not in fear of rejection but in the truth of being loved and chosen by God? What step could begin that shift today?

9

Healing Begins with Telling

WHEN TRUTH IS SPOKEN, shame begins to lose its power. Silence allows secrets to grow heavy, but bringing our stories into trusted spaces lets them breathe. Naming what happened—and how it has shaped us—separates our identity from our wounds. We are not what was done to us; we are the ones who endured and still stand.

In the room, telling unfolds slowly: a sentence, a pause, a breath. Choice returns—What do I share? How much today? With whom?—and the nervous system learns that truth can be spoken without punishment. Fragments begin to link: this memory to that feeling, this reaction to that loss. Coherence is a kind of mercy.

Spiritually, telling is agreeing with God's truth about our lives. Scripture calls this confession—not groveling, but speaking honestly. When truth is spoken, God meets us there with kindness. Light doesn't scold the dark; it just enters. Telling becomes an act of courage that begins to break shame's hold.

Secrecy keeps shame alive; truth brings light. In therapy, each honest word helps the nervous system find a little more ground, and relationship becomes more possible. This chapter holds space for that kind of telling—the kind that neither minimizes the wound nor magnifies the offender, but honors your story and points it toward healing.

Here we consider what telling looks like clinically and spiritually: naming the past without living there, linking symptoms to roots, inviting God's presence into the places that still ache, and practicing small, embodied steps that make safety feel possible again. With that frame in place, we listen to one woman who chose to tell.

One Client's Story: Simone (pseudonym)

Presenting Problem: Simone came to therapy carrying a long history of fear and fragmentation. Anxiety was her constant companion, often overwhelming her ability to function. At times she dissociated, retreating inward when life felt too threatening to face. Beneath these symptoms lay the scars of domestic violence—years of living in a home where safety was shattered and trust was broken.

Diagnosis: Simone met the criteria for Generalized Anxiety Disorder (GAD), with excessive worry, restlessness, and difficulty concentrating that touched nearly every area of her life. She also carried symptoms of Post-Traumatic Stress Disorder (PTSD)—flashbacks, hypervigilance, and a startle response that reminded her that the past was never fully past.

Narrative

Simone was thirty-seven when she entered therapy. She had recently fled an abusive relationship and was living with a friend. Her voice trembled as she spoke—both from fear and from the effort it took to tell her story. "I've never really had a place of my own," she said quietly. "I mean, I've lived places. . . but none of them felt safe."

Her earliest memories carried that same theme of unsafe spaces. Though her grandmother had raised her from birth, Simone carried the wound of rejection from her mother, who had given her away so she could "live her best life." The implicit message was rejection—a message reinforced years later when her mother disclosed she had never wanted to carry the pregnancy to term. Simone's biological father, whom she never met, was married to another woman at the time. The pregnancy itself was difficult, and her mother admitted she had even considered abortion. Simone was carried to term, but not carried in love—and those early months of rejection left an imprint that followed her into adulthood.

Though Simone lived with her grandmother, weekends with her mother left a different kind of mark. What should have been times of connection became scenes of chaos, filled with shouting and violence between her mother and boyfriend. Those early exposures planted a script of instability and fear.

What she first witnessed in her mother's home—domestic violence, volatility, and abandonment—eventually became part of her own lived reality. Drawn into relationships marked by the same chaos, Simone found herself repeating the cycle. What had once been her mother's pain had now become her own.

And yet, her grandmother planted a different seed. From an early age, she enrolled Simone in dance classes, and movement became a lifeline. The studio offered her something the home never did: freedom. In dance, Simone discovered expression when words failed her and strength when fear threatened to silence her. Over the years, it became a thread of continuity, reminding her that beauty could exist even in the midst of chaos.

By her early twenties, Simone sought out counseling. Therapy became her first safe place to begin untangling the web of pain. "The therapist helped me find out what it was and what the causes were and how to relate things to my childhood," she explained. Over time, she learned to connect the anxiety and numbness she carried in the present with the wounds of her past. "The Bible is very helpful, incredibly helpful. . . with getting through everything I had to go through," she said. I suspected Simone respected Scripture, yet it had not captured her heart in a way that brought lasting peace. Faith gave her language, but not yet the felt safety she longed for.

Beneath the surface, fear still ruled her inner world—fear of intimacy, fear of being unworthy, fear of trusting others or even God. In private, her anxiety was relentless. She endured nightmares, panic attacks, and dissociation. "I don't think I even know what calm feels like," she admitted. When asked what she wanted most from therapy, Simone paused for a long time, then whispered words that carried the weight of her life's longing: "I just want to feel safe somewhere."

Psychological Insight

Simone's trauma narrative revealed not only the impact of her own experiences but also the echoes of generational trauma. What she first witnessed in her mother's home—domestic violence, volatility, and abandonment—later became patterns in her own intimate relationships. As trauma researcher Dr. Bessel van der Kolk explains, trauma is not just a past event—it is an experience that overwhelms the nervous system and continues to live in the body as if the danger were still happening.

For Simone, the nervous system she carried had been shaped in an environment where love and violence coexisted, and where rejection was woven into her beginning.

Generational trauma is rarely linear, but it is persistent. Simone's mother, burdened by her own unhealed wounds, could not nurture her child in safety. Instead, the cycle of chaos and violence continued into Simone's adulthood, replaying the familiar script of instability. This helps us see her struggles not as isolated weaknesses but as part of a larger family story—one that had gone unnamed for too long.

Layered onto this was the wound of being unwanted before she was even born. Research shows that when a mother is conflicted or distressed about her pregnancy, the fetus absorbs that stress in utero. This primal rejection often imprints itself into the child's developing sense of self, later surfacing as anxiety, depression, and attachment difficulties.

Simone's struggles, then, were not signs of weakness—they were embodied echoes of her story. She was not merely remembering her past; she was reliving it, over and over again, through her body and her relationships. The constant anxiety and dissociation she described were not personality flaws but the residue of trauma—her body's way of trying to survive what her soul had never been given space to heal.

Insight as Therapist–Interviewer

Sitting with Simone was a lesson in patience and presence. Her story did not come out in neat sequences but in fragments—starts and stops, silence and trembling. As a therapist, my role was less about "fixing" and more about holding a steady, non-judgmental space where safety could slowly grow. I learned that the pace of telling is as important as the telling itself; every pause was its own act of courage.

What struck me most was how deeply Simone longed for safety and how she risked trusting me with her story despite years of betrayal. Bearing witness to her pain reminded me that healing is not a technique but a relationship—one where dignity is restored not by rushing the process but by accompanying someone until hope begins to flicker again.

Spiritual Insight

Simone's story revealed a gap between knowing Scripture and experiencing its refuge. Her head held verses, but her body still carried fear. Spiritually, this is the space where theology meets trauma—the place where God's promises must move from concept to encounter.

Together we began to name the distinction between trauma and God's presence. Trauma startles and exposes; it keeps the body braced for impact. God's presence, by contrast, steadies. It offers a covering—a quiet invitation to safety that starts within, softening the body's reflex to expect harm. Trauma reopens old wounds; God binds them. Trauma screams "You are alone"; God whispers, "You are known."

Psalm 91 names this paradoxical refuge: a secret place under the shadow of the Almighty. That shelter is less about architecture and more about relationship. It is in the steady nearness of another—God's faithful presence—that the wounded can begin to rest, not because the storm is gone but because they do not face it alone.

Slowly, with patient and compassionate repair, Simone began to imagine a God who was different from the people who had abandoned her. She began to consider that perhaps God had been present all along—quietly, persistently, waiting for her to learn that safety could be found in His arms.

Note from the Father's Heart

Daughter,

I have heard you ask, "If you are my Father, why didn't you protect me?" That question lived in my hearing long before you spoke it. I know how abandonment has clouded your view of Me—but I am not like those who left you.

When fear silenced your voice, I was listening.

You were never invisible to Me.

I am your shelter, not your accuser.

I am your refuge, not your abandoner.

I am your peace, not your fear.

You do not need to run to unsafe places in search of safety.

Come to Me. Let Me show you that I never left and I never will.

In My presence you are chosen.

You are wanted.

You are wholly Mine.

—Jesus

Hope Woven Into the Frame

Simone's story reminds us that even when rejection and violence have left deep marks, healing is still possible. Every step she took toward telling her story was a thread of hope—proof that silence does not have the final word. What began as fragmented memories slowly became a coherent narrative, one she could hold without being consumed by it.

Her willingness to risk trust again—to sit in the safety of the counseling room, to return to Scripture with new openness—shows that hope is not found in the absence of fear but in the choice to reach for light anyway. For others who carry similar wounds, Simone's journey testifies that healing unfolds slowly, but it unfolds. Every sentence spoken, every tear released, every breath of truth is a stitch in a new story—one not defined by rejection, but by restoration.

Follow-Up

Simone remains in therapy and continues to contend with the ache of being dismissed and misunderstood. Naming the origins of her pain—including the ways rejection reached back into the womb— has given her a language to describe long-held disconnection and, with that language, a pathway into repair.

Though she continues to wrestle with self-doubt and a tendency to over-function, Simone is learning small practices that reshape experience: pausing when panic rises, practicing stillness despite the urge to flee, and setting boundaries that protect her body and heart. These are not dramatic fixes but steady, relational shifts that, over time, change the wiring of fear into the capacity for rest. Her journey is unfinished, but she is no longer hiding. She is beginning to receive love that does not need proof, to speak her needs without apology, and to imagine a different legacy for herself and for those who will come after her.

Reflective Questions

1. Have you ever longed for emotional safety but struggled to find it? How did that longing shape your choices or relationships?

2. What does "safe" mean to you in this season of your life, and where—if anywhere—do you experience it now?

3. In what ways have you tried to protect yourself from being hurt again? Have those protections brought peace, or have they left you feeling more isolated?

4. Who or what has begun to feel like a true refuge on your journey? How might you lean more deeply into that place of safety?

10

The One Who Always Wanted Me

Trauma is more than a wound—it is a disruption. A tear in the fabric of one's identity, one's story, one's safety. It lingers long after the moment has passed—etched into the nervous system, woven into relationships, silently embedded in how we see ourselves, others, and even God.

Clinically, trauma is understood as an emotional response to a distressing or overwhelming experience—something that exceeds the brain and body's ability to cope. It may come through a single event like abuse or abandonment, or emerge from chronic conditions such as emotional neglect, instability, or prolonged rejection.

But trauma is not only psychological. It is holistic. It imprints itself on the body, distorts belief systems, and fragments the soul. It doesn't always lead to a diagnosis, but it always leaves residue. And for those who experience trauma early in life—especially in the womb or early childhood—the effects can be devastating. These individuals often grow up carrying a fractured sense of self, shaped not by truth, but by survival.

Perhaps the most insidious form of trauma is the one we inherit. Generational trauma is the silent inheritance that passed from one generation to the next. It is the grief, shame, and fear that parents unknowingly hand down to their children—like broken heirlooms wrapped in silence. When trauma is inherited—when a parent passes down their own emotional wounding, consciously or unconsciously—the impact becomes even more complex. The child shoulders not only their own pain but also the unresolved anguish of those who came before them.

This chapter explores the life of Naomi, a woman shaped by rejection, longing, and the weight of generational pain. For Naomi, trauma came early—and it stayed too long.

One Client's Story: Naomi (pseudonym)

Presenting Problem: Naomi entered therapy carrying layers of unspoken grief and inner conflict. Chronic sadness shadowed her daily life, often tipping into despair. Emotional detachment left her feeling numb and disconnected, even in relationships where she longed for closeness. Her inner dialogue was marked by self-hatred, reinforced by a history of maternal rejection and severe abandonment wounds.

Diagnosis: Naomi's clinical picture aligned with Major Depressive Disorder, characterized by pervasive sadness, hopelessness, and diminished interest in life. Beneath this diagnosis, however, lay features of Complex Post-Traumatic Stress Disorder (C-PTSD)—the accumulated impact of prolonged childhood trauma and rejection. Symptoms of hypervigilance, intrusive memories, and emotional dysregulation reflected unresolved trauma woven throughout her story.

Narrative

I chose the name Naomi after the woman in Scripture whose story was marked by deep loss and sorrow. In her grief she said, "Don't call me Naomi; call me Mara, for the Lord has dealt bitterly with me." I understood those words. For many years, bitterness felt like my name too—something I wore like an identity. I often wondered, *Why has life been so unkind?*

Even as a Christian, I was deeply miserable. Yet I clung to the promise that the good work God had begun in me, He would be faithful to complete. That hope became my lifeline. Still, I had no name for the years of self-loathing, heartache, and pain. I only knew the weight of it, and I feared I was doomed to live in a cycle of sorrow. In those years, my prayer often echoed the words of the Apostle Paul: "O wretched man that I am, who shall deliver me from this body of death and sorrow?" (Romans 7:24). Others could see what I was carrying, even when I couldn't name it myself. One day, as I walked down the street, my mother turned to my daughter and said, "Here comes your mother, mad at the world." Her words stung because they were true. Anger had become the mask I wore, but beneath it was despair.

When I first received Christ as my Lord and Savior, I believed life would change instantly—that joy would replace sorrow and all the old wounds would disappear—but I came to Him carrying all my baggage: emotional wounds, disappointments, failures, self-hatred, and an inability to receive His goodness for my life. I thought I had to earn His love, and the striving left me weary, disillusioned, and exhausted.

Before I ever discovered the wound of prenatal rejection, another buried truth surfaced. Around the age of forty, I came to realize that I had been sexually violated. The remembrance of the event had been hidden deep within me, but its impact was unmistakable. My personality shifted almost overnight, and everyone in the family noticed. My behavior changed, my spirit carried a heaviness, and though I could not name the source, the wound was already shaping me.

I understand now that the mind sometimes protects itself by suppressing trauma until a person is strong enough to face it. But even when hidden, trauma still speaks—through the body, through behavior, and through the heaviness carried in the soul.

When I uncovered the violation, I thought, *Now things will begin to shift.* But awareness alone did not bring healing. The memories explained some of my pain, but they did not untangle the deeper wound that ran through my life.

It wasn't until prenatal rejection was named—the true root—that change began to take hold. After years of inner struggle—self-hatred, disappointment, setbacks, and broken relationships—I finally heard the words that gave my pain a name. It happened at a church conference on a Saturday evening. The gathering was called *Leaving Your Past Behind*, and to me, that sounded like exactly what I needed. In the midst of the service, a prayer was offered and we were invited to the altar. As I stood there, the pastor pointed at me and declared: "It started in the womb. The rejection started in the womb. And now that the root has been disclosed, healing will begin to emerge in your life." Those words pierced me. For the first time, what I had carried all my life had a name—and healing no longer felt like a distant dream.

In the days that followed, memories of other moments of prayer began to resurface. I remembered being told to receive healing for the wound of rejection. I recalled a pastor pausing mid-service to say he saw the Lord placing a big, warm covering over me to bring healing. These were tender images, but at the time I didn't fully grasp how deeply rejection had shaped my life. It wasn't until that altar call that everything came into focus.

Soon after, I began to understand why so much of my life had felt fractured. My bond with my mother had never truly been present. Though she was physically there, emotionally we did not connect. For years I couldn't explain it—now I knew.

The same struggle echoed in my own motherhood. My attachment with my children had always felt strained, as if something invisible stood in the way. Looking back, I can now see where it began.

With my firstborn, the wound revealed itself in the delivery room. When the nurse asked if I wanted to hold her, I quietly whispered, "No, not now." Days passed before I finally looked at her as she lay in the incubator. The rejection deepened when her father left to start a new family with someone else. My second child's story was different, yet connected. I received her when she was born, but not during the time I carried her. For nine months she grew inside me, but my heart had turned away.

My rejection of my children was not an isolated event. I, too, had come into the world unwanted—as had my mother before me. The wound stretched back through generations, passed down like an unspoken inheritance. I carried not only my own pain but also the weight of rejection etched into my family line.

Now I finally understood why so much had felt disconnected, both in my upbringing and in my motherhood. The rejection that began in the womb had reached across generations, quietly shaping how love was given and received. Naming it was painful, but it was also the beginning of freedom.

Psychological Insight

My story reveals the devastating ripple effects of prenatal rejection and unprocessed trauma. Developmental psychologist Erik Erikson emphasized the importance of the earliest stages of life—particularly *Trust vs. Mistrust* and *Autonomy vs. Shame and Doubt*. For me, those core needs for security, affirmation, and belonging were never met. The result was not only mistrust of others, but also mistrust of myself—my worth, my goodness, and even my ability to be loved.

Abraham Maslow's hierarchy of needs identifies love and belonging as critical once basic survival is secured. Yet that need was never truly filled for me. Rejection from the womb shaped my worldview and my self-concept. What looked like promiscuity on the surface was never about pleasure; it was protest. A search. A desperate attempt to matter to someone.

My inability to bond with my children reflected not indifference but an interrupted attachment system—an early template of disconnection carried forward into motherhood. This is how generational trauma perpetuates itself: pain passed down silently, yet powerfully, from one generation to the next.

And beneath it all lay cognitive distortions—beliefs such as *I'm unlovable. I'm unworthy. I am the black sheep of the family.* These were not just fleeting thoughts; they were identity markers etched into my body and soul. Only when those markers were named, grieved, and replaced with truth did the cycle begin to lose its grip.

Insight as Therapist–Interviewer

As I sat for this interview, I realized I was both the one asking the questions and the one whose story was unfolding. Listening to myself through this process gave me a rare perspective—holding my pain with the awareness of a therapist, yet also feeling it as the one who had lived it. The interview became a mirror, reflecting the generational rejection I had carried and giving language to the silent wounds that shaped me.

My story revealed how trauma can hide in plain sight until it's named. For years, I carried the weight of sadness without understanding its root, until one night I dreamed I was pulling weeds in a garden. As I worked, I heard a voice say, "You have to pull up the roots, because weeds can grow back." That dream captured what I did not yet have words for: it was not enough to trim away symptoms or silence my sadness. The roots of rejection had to be named and uprooted, or else they would return again and again.

This is why telling matters. Healing begins the moment the hidden roots are brought into the light, when silence is broken and truth is spoken. For me, the interview was not only research—it was revelation.

Note to the Reader

The story you just read was especially heavy for me to share. My journey bears the weight of trauma, prenatal rejection, and generational wounds that shaped much of my life. I did not tell it to magnify despair but to uncover the hidden reality of wounds that often go unseen.

If parts of my story stirred pain in your own, know that you are not alone. The same God who met me in the deepest places of rejection is present for you as well. His love does not turn away from our brokenness; it leans in, steady and sure, offering healing where we least expect it.

My prayer is that as you reflect on what you've read, you will hear His voice in your own story—the voice that says, *"You are loved, you are chosen, and you are Mine."*

Spiritual Insight

For many years, I struggled to believe that God truly loved me. Once, in desperation, I went to a pastor and confessed, "I just want to hear God say He loves me." The pastor gently replied, "He is saying it now." But I couldn't receive it. The words slipped past my wounded heart.

Rejection is not only psychological—it is spiritual. It leaves an open wound the enemy eagerly exploits. In my case, generational rejection carved a deep spiritual wound. My mother hadn't chosen me, and unknowingly, I repeated the pattern by failing to bond with my own children. This wasn't malice; it was inherited pain—an unspoken legacy of unworthiness passed down through generations.

After coming to Christ, I was drawn to the book of Ephesians, where Paul prayed that we might grasp "how wide and long and high and deep is the love of Christ." That verse became a lifeline. I longed for that kind of love—vast, pure, healing. Yet without inner healing, the love I sought was often a poor substitute: fleeting affection that left me emptier than before, validation that evaporated by morning.

Eventually, I realized I couldn't untangle these wounds on my own. In time, I found myself sitting in the quiet space of counseling, unsure of what to expect but desperate for change. After listening to my story, a Christian counselor looked me in the eye and said, "Naomi, you have believed lies about yourself, about others, and about God." *Whoa.* It was as if scales fell from my heart and ears. I realized that healing meant more than naming my pain—it required exchanging lies for truth. But whose truth? Jesus declared, "You shall know the truth, and the truth shall make you free." Slowly, I began surrendering sorrow, fear, and unworthiness in exchange for the unchanging truth of God's Word.

Ironically, I had once insisted, "Black people don't go to therapy." And yet there I was—week after week—being undone and remade in the presence of Christ. Today, as a clinical social worker myself, I can only marvel: only God could have written that twist in my story.

Note from the Father's Heart

My precious Naomi,

Before you were formed in the womb, I knew you. I shaped you with intention, and you were never a mistake. I saw the rejection that shadowed your beginning, but even then you were Mine—never too much, never forgotten.

Even as a little one, I walked beside you. The enemy tried to silence you with heartache, with pain, with self-hatred and lies, but his words were never the final word. Through every shadow, I was there, keeping you, holding you, whispering truth when you could not yet hear it.

I watched when sorrow tried to overwhelm you, when betrayal cut deeply, when shame told you that you were ruined. Yet I never turned away. Those wounds do not disqualify you from My love; they are the very places where My grace runs deepest.

Where there were ashes, I am bringing forth beauty. Where there were tears, I am bringing forth peace. Every layer of pain is being lifted, one by one, until your heart rests secure in My love.

After all, "love me" was the cry of your heart. And I say to you now: I have always loved you, with an everlasting love. You belong to Me. I rejoice over you with singing, I quiet you with My love, and I delight in you with gladness.

You are not Mara, marked by bitterness. You are Naomi—
pleasant, chosen, and Mine. Your story is not over—I am rewriting it
with hope, with restoration, and with everlasting love.
      —Jesus

Hope Woven Into the Frame

If my life tells you anything, let it tell you this: trauma does not get
the final say. Rejection may have written my first chapters, but it
does not hold the pen anymore. God does.

What I once carried as shame, He has turned into testimony. The emptiness that haunted me has become the very place
His presence fills. The ache for love I could never seem to find has
been answered in Him—the God who calls me chosen, wanted,
and His own.

And here is what I've come to know: healing is a journey, not a
single event. It unfolds in its own time, and there is no need to rush
the process. God whispers, *"Trust that I am at work, even in your*
pain, and I will bring all things together for your good. You will be
sustained, carried, and rescued. You will not be forgotten." The story
He rewrote for me is the story He stands ready to rewrite for you.

Follow-Up

I now attend family counseling, and my relationship with my
children has improved greatly. For years I lived at a distance from
them, but therapy has opened space for new conversations and
small steps toward connection. For so long, pain and sorrow were
my closest companions. But now, I am learning to welcome new
companions—grace and mercy. By naming the rejection I carried
from the womb, I have begun to grieve what I never received and
to invite God into those empty places.

My healing is unfolding like an onion, peeled layer by layer—
each one bringing me into greater awareness and releasing me from
the shadow of shame. Along the way, I graduated from college,

established a nonprofit agency to serve those who are broken and bruised, and authored several books on emotional wellness. I am finally learning what it means to enjoy life.

And this is the hope for every wounded heart: what begins in silence and sorrow can become the very place where truth breaks through. The God who seemed absent in my darkest moments is the same God who had never left—and who has always wanted me.

Reflective Questions

1. What was your earliest experience of feeling unloved, unseen, or unsafe?

2. Have you ever carried emotional pain that seemed to belong to someone before you?

3. How do you define love today—and is that definition shaped more by truth or by trauma?

4. What would it look like to begin breaking the cycle of generational trauma in your family?

11

An Invitation to Healing

Naming the Root

BEFORE HEALING CAN TAKE hold, we must name the root of our pain. This is not merely a spiritual idea; both psychology and trauma recovery affirm it. Unnamed pain festers. Unacknowledged wounds continue to shape thoughts, emotions, and behavior long after the original event has passed.

- Psychology shows that recurring emotional patterns often grow out of deeply held core beliefs such as *"I am unlovable"* or *"I am a failure."* Healing begins when these hidden beliefs are brought to light and gently challenged.

- Trauma recovery teaches that pain that remains unspoken lingers in the body and nervous system. Naming the event and its impact allows the brain and body to re-establish a sense of safety.

- Spiritual formation calls this confession—not groveling, but "saying the same" as God says. Honest acknowledgment opens the way for repentance, forgiveness, and restoration.

Think of it like a splinter beneath the skin: you can bandage the surface as much as you want, but until the splinter is found and removed, the infection remains. Naming the ache is a sacred act of truth-telling. It validates experience, dismantles denial, and gives language to the cries of the soul. For many of the people whose stories fill these pages—and in my own story—the root was prenatal rejection: a wound carried silently from the womb.

Over time, other experiences—abuse, abandonment, shame—layered on top of that early mark. The soul became a vault where trauma was stored, locked away, hidden from sight, but never beyond God's reach. It is into that vault, the deepest part of us, that He longs to enter with His healing.

Soul Wounds and God's Answer

Soul wounds are more than insecurities or passing sorrows. They are deep imprints left when love is withheld, belonging is fractured, or joy is stolen before it can take root. These wounds can begin as early as the womb and are compounded through experiences such as:

- Abandonment by parents or caregivers
- Physical, emotional, or sexual trauma
- Humiliation and persistent shame
- Betrayal by those who should have been safe
- Unresolved grief and loss
- Injustice and the corrosive weight of living in a broken world

Psychologically, these experiences shape attachment patterns, self-concept, and emotional regulation. Spiritually, they often become places where lies take root: *"I'm alone." "I'm unworthy." "I'm unlovable."* These wounds often disguise themselves as strength—through independence, perfectionism, over-functioning, or even hyper-spiritual activity—but beneath the surface, they cry out to be seen. Left unnamed, they lock the soul's door with shame and silence.

And here is the hope: God does not leave wounds untended. *"He restores my soul"* (Psalm 23:3). *"He binds up the brokenhearted"* (Isaiah 61:1). The vault does not remain closed forever. In gentleness and unfailing kindness, God turns the key—not to expose us in weakness, but to heal us in our brokenness. Where trauma once spoke *"You are unwanted,"* God speaks a truer word:

- "You are chosen."
- "You are loved with an everlasting love."
- "You are Mine."

What was once hidden can become the place where His presence dwells; what was once tangled with shame can be rewoven with grace.

A Pathway into Healing

Naming the root opens the way, but naming alone is not enough. Scripture warns against leaving an empty space that something worse might fill (Matthew 12:43–45). Healing is a movement of replacement—removing the lie and planting truth in its place. Both psychological and spiritual transformation require active participation. The following pathway is simple but profound:

1. Name it. Identify the root ache and the lie it has whispered over your life. Bringing it into conscious awareness disrupts its hidden power.

2. Grieve it. Allow what comes. Tears are not weakness; they are part of the healing flow. Trauma work affirms that grieving is necessary for integration.

3. Surrender it. Place the wound into God's hands. He is big enough to hold what you cannot carry. Receive truth. Let Scripture and the Spirit replace the lies. Where you once heard, *"You are unwanted,"* hear the voice that says, *"You are*

Mine." Philippians 4:8 offers a guide for reorienting the mind toward what is true, noble, and good.

4. Walk in support. Healing often unfolds in relationship—with a trusted counselor, a faithful community, and the Holy Spirit guiding each step. Healthy attachment experiences in the present can reshape old patterns from the past.

Scriptures to Hold

- "Though my father and mother forsake me, the Lord will receive me."—Psalm 27:10
- "I have loved you with an everlasting love; I have drawn you with unfailing kindness."—Jeremiah 31:3
- "He chose us in Him before the foundation of the world. . . In love He predestined us for adoption to sonship."—Ephesians 1:4–5
- "The Lord is close to the brokenhearted and saves those who are crushed in spirit."—Psalm 34:18
- "Nothing. . . will be able to separate us from the love of God that is in Christ Jesus our Lord."—Romans 8:39

Reflective Questions

1. What lie have I carried that I need to surrender to God?
2. Where do I sense God inviting me to open the vault of my soul?
3. What loss or wound am I ready to grieve with Him?
4. What new word of truth do I most need to receive today?
5. How might my healing influence the next generation in my family?

A Closing Prayer

Lord, I bring You the hidden vaults of my soul. I name before You the lies I have believed and the pain I have carried.

I surrender them into Your hands
and ask You to replace them with Your truth.

Thank You for choosing me, loving me, and calling me Your own.

Heal what has been wounded,
restore what has been lost,
and rewrite my story with Your love.

Amen.

Final Benediction

You are no longer unseen.
You are no longer unheard.
You are welcomed, cherished, delighted in, and forever wanted.

Go in peace—
held by the One who has always loved you and who still sings over you today.

Closing Vision

Healing is like a garden. For years the weeds may grow unchecked—choking joy, blocking light, and hiding beauty. But when the Gardener steps in, He does not despise the overgrowth. With patience and care, He uproots what does not belong and replants what was lost. In time, the ground that once bore thorns begins to bear fruit.

This is the promise: your healing is not only for you. When one life is restored, families shift. When families shift, generations shift. And when generations shift, communities begin to heal. What God heals in you can ripple in ways you may not see this side of eternity. This is His promise: "Behold, I am making all things new." (Revelation 21:5)

For years, I only called Him 'God.' But now, He is my Father—the Dad I never had. I am His daughter.

An Invitation to Healing

My Letter to My Heavenly Father

My Heavenly Father,

I thank You that You see every part of me—the places that have been wounded, the walls that were built for protection, and the deep longing in my heart to know and be known.

I acknowledge that my early wounds affected how I related to You and to others. But I refuse to live defined by that old story any longer.

Today, I choose to trust Your promise to heal and restore the parts of my life that were damaged and stolen. You are rewriting my heart with love, stability, and belonging. I open my heart to intimacy with You—not cautiously, but fully. I give You permission to touch the places I once hid. I welcome healthy, Spirit-led connections into my life. I declare that I am safe, worthy of love, and able to give and receive it freely.

My identity is not "wounded," but "restored." My story is not "abandoned," but "redeemed." My heart is no longer guarded by fear, but held by perfect Love.

Father, I am so grateful. There was a time I believed I would always be broken—marked by soul wounds, disappointments, condemnation, regrets, and self-hatred. But You have proven Yourself faithful. You are healing me fully and completely. You are the Dad I never had, and I am Your daughter. In Jesus' name, I step into the fullness of healing You've prepared for me.

Love,
Your daughter

An Invitation to Healing

As you close this book, may this moment become your "yes" to God's healing. The wounds of the past do not define the future. The final word over your life belongs to the One who has always wanted you. His invitation still stands: let Him touch the places that have been hidden—the wounds carried too long, the lies believed too deeply. The ache you carry, the questions you've asked, the silence you've endured—none of these are too heavy for Him.

Healing does not erase the past; it allows God to write the final word. And that word is not rejection, abandonment, or shame. It is love. It is belonging. It is *new*. Hold fast to this truth: "Behold, I am making all things new" (Revelation 21:5).

Bibliography

Ainsworth, Mary D. Salter, Mary C. Blehar, Everett Waters, and Sally Wall. *Patterns of Attachment: A Psychological Study of the Strange Situation.* Hillsdale, NJ: Erlbaum, 1978.

Altman, M. R., T. Oseguera, M. R. McLemore, I. Kantrowitz-Gordon, L. S. Franck, and A. Lyndon. "Information and Power: Women of Color's Experiences Interacting with Health Care Providers in Pregnancy and Birth." *Social Science & Medicine* 270 (2021): 113674. https://doi.org/10.1016/j.socscimed.2021.113674.

Baumrind, Diana. "Effects of Authoritative Parental Control on Child Behavior." *Child Development* 37, no. 4 (1966): 887–907.

———. "Current Patterns of Parental Authority." *Developmental Psychology Monograph* 4, no. 1, pt. 2 (1971): 1–103.

Bibring, Grete, Donald W. Dwyer, Josephine D. Huntington, and W. B. Valenstein. "A Study of the Psychological Processes in Pregnancy and of the Earliest Mother–Child Relationship." *The Psychoanalytic Study of the Child* 16 (1961): 9–24.

Bowlby, John. *Attachment and Loss: Vol. 1. Attachment.* New York: Basic, 1969.

Centers for Disease Control and Prevention (CDC). "Racial and Ethnic Disparities in Maternal Mortality." National Center for Health Statistics, 2022. https://www.cdc.gov/nchs/maternal-mortality/.

Cherry, Kendra. "Unintended Pregnancies and Their Effects on Children." *Verywell Mind.* Last updated March 21, 2023. https://www.verywellmind.com/unintended-pregnancies-and-their-effects-on-children-5185081.

Chiu, Elizabeth, Isaac Maddow-Zimet, and Kathryn Kost. "Unintended and Unwanted Pregnancy in the United States, 2012–2017." Guttmacher Institute, 2024. https://www.guttmacher.org/report/unintended-unwanted-pregnancy-us-2012-2017.

Cortizo, R. "The Calming Womb Family Therapy Model: Bonding Mother and Baby from Pregnancy Forward." *Journal of Prenatal & Perinatal Psychology & Health* 33, no. 3 (2019): 207–20.

David, Henry P., Zdeněk Dytrych, Zdeněk Matějček, and Václav Schüller. *Born Unwanted: Developmental Effects of Denied Abortion.* New York: Springer, 1988.

———. "Born Unwanted 25 Years Later: The Prague Study." *Reproductive Health Matters* 14, no. 27 (2006): 181–90.

Dominguez, T. P. "Adverse Birth Outcomes in African American Women: The Social Context of Persistent Reproductive Disadvantage." *Social Work in Public Health* 25, no. 1 (2010): 3–16. https://doi.org/10.1080/19371910902989412.

Erikson, Erik H. *Identity: Youth and Crisis.* New York: Norton, 1968.

Foster, Diana Greene. *The Turnaway Study: Ten Years, a Thousand Women, and the Consequences of Having—or Being Denied—an Abortion.* New York: Scribner, 2020.

Fraiberg, Selma, Edna Adelson, and Vivian Shapiro. "Ghosts in the Nursery: A Psychoanalytic Approach to the Problems of Impaired Infant–Mother Relationships." *Journal of the American Academy of Child Psychiatry* 14, no. 3 (1975): 387–421.

Kalsched, Donald. *Trauma and the Soul: A Psycho-Spiritual Approach to Human Development and Its Interruption.* London: Routledge, 2013.

Maslow, Abraham H. Motivation and Personality. New York: Harper & Row, 1954.

Maslow, Abraham H. "A Theory of Human Motivation." *Psychological Review* 50, no. 4 (1943): 370–96.

Piaget, Jean. *The Language and Thought of the Child.* Translated by Marjorie Gabain and Ruth Gabain. New York: Harcourt, Brace & Company, 1926.

Reardon, David C., and Jesse R. Cougle. "Depression and Unintended Pregnancy in the National Longitudinal Survey of Youth: A Cohort Study." *BMJ* 324, no. 7330 (2002): 151–52. https://doi.org/10.1136/bmj.324.7330.151.

Sivaraman, V. S., Harish Thippeswamy, Mariamma Philip, Geetha Desai, and Prabha Chandra. "Is Maternal-Fetal Attachment Affected in Women with Severe Mental Illness?" *Journal of Prenatal & Perinatal Psychology & Health* 32 (2018): 306–18.

van der Kolk, Bessel. *The Body Keeps the Score: Brain, Mind, and Body in the Healing of Trauma.* New York: Viking, 2014.

van IJzendoorn, M. H. "Adult Attachment Representations, Parental Responsiveness, and Infant Attachment: A Meta-Analysis on the Predictive Validity of the Adult Attachment Interview." *Psychological Bulletin* 117, no. 3 (1995): 387–403. https://doi.org/10.1037/0033-2909.117.3.387.

Van Eijsden, Manon, T. G. M. Vrijkotte, R. J. B. J. Gemke, and M. F. van der Wal. "Cohort Profile: The Amsterdam Born Children and Their Development (ABCD) Study." *International Journal of Epidemiology* 40, no. 5 (2011): 1176–1186. https://doi.org/10.1093/ije/dyq128.

Verny, Thomas, and John Kelly. The Secret Life of the Unborn Child. New York: Delta, 1981.

Bibliography

Verny, T. R., and P. Weintraub. *Nurturing the Unborn Child: A Nine-Month Program for Soothing, Stimulating, and Communicating with Your Baby.* New York: Delacorte, 2002.

Winnicott, D. W. *The Maturational Processes and the Facilitating Environment.* London: Hogarth, 1965.

Yehuda, Rachel, et al. "Holocaust Exposure Induced Intergenerational Effects on FKBP5 Methylation." Biological Psychiatry 80, no. 5 (2016): 372–380.

Yehuda, R., N. P. Daskalakis, A. Lehrner, F. Desarnaud, H. N. Bader, I. Makotkine, . . . and M. J. Meaney. "Influences of Maternal and Paternal PTSD on Epigenetic Regulation of the Glucocorticoid Receptor Gene in Holocaust Survivor Offspring." *American Journal of Psychiatry* 171, no. 8 (2016): 872–80. https://doi.org/10.1176/appi.ajp.2014.13121571.